Advance Praise for *Challenges for Today's Living*

This is an extraordinary book. As a pastor, I often preached from Paul's letters to the Corinthians, but I now realize that I could have done it far more effectively if I had had Bill Tuck's book to help me understand what Paul was saying and why he was saying it the way he did. I salute you, Bill, for what is perhaps the finest book you ever wrote! And my advice to every pastor is to get this book and read it as soon as you have it in your hands.

—**John Killinger**
Former professor, Vanderbilt Divinity School
Former pastor, First Congregational Church of Los Angeles
Author of more than fifty books

I am downright eager to say a good word for this highly relevant book on 1 Corinthians. It is written not only intelligently but with the creativity of a homiletics professor and seasoned pastor. This is not merely a good addition to your bookcase as a reference work but also a dynamic resource for a series of sermons or lessons or personal devotions. It is informed not only exegetically for the text but also the times. This book speaks to the ethics of Paul with its spectacular practicality and to the theology of Paul, who was among other things a gifted intellectual.

—**Peter Rhea Jones**
Professor Emeritus of New Testament
McAfee School of Theology
Former pastor, First Baptist Church, Decatur, Georgia

Dr. William Tuck's lovely book about 1 Corinthians, like a Swiss army knife, has several possible uses. You can read it for its practical advice about Christian living. You can read it as devotional meditations. You can read it to learn what Bible scholars have been saying about St. Paul's great letter. You can read it as an anthology of delightful stories, some touching and others humorous. You can read it for its careful analysis of complex issues the church faces today. I recommend it wholeheartedly to ministers and laypeople alike.

—**Fisher Humphreys**
ır of Divinity Emeritus, Samford University
Birmingham, Alabama

D1484006

Our present day is marked by massive faction and division. The various threads that once held our society together have become irreparably frayed. No part of life has been immune to its effects, unfortunately not even the church. Nonetheless, Christians possess the inspired words of the Apostle Paul, who spoke God's truth to a similarly challenged people on the verge of seeing their witness for Christ grind to a halt. Paul's first letter to the Corinthians is a trove of both theological and practical counsel for a people who had much to offer Christ's cause in the first century world. In *Challenges for Today's Living*, Bill Tuck unpacks the themes that Paul employed to get the believers in that strategic city back on track in pursuit of "the more excellent way." Whether one comes to these studies as a struggling disciple or as a member of a local congregation that is reeling from the difficulties that inevitably befall communities of all types, Tuck's insights into Paul's direction will provide much-needed encouragement and inspiration and, more importantly, a path forward toward a reclaimed future in which everyone finds his or her place as a valued member of the Body of Christ.

—Doug Dortch
Pastor, Mountain Brook Baptist Church
Birmingham, Alabama

In *Challenges for Today's Living: Studies in 1 Corinthians*, the Rev. Dr. William Powell Tuck unpacks key themes in the Apostle Paul's letter, ranging from major areas of Christian theology to the practical aspects of living in Christian community. With his characteristic insight informed by his years as both a pastor and a scholar, Tuck brings to life the relevancy of Paul's instruction in 1 Corinthians for the life of Christians today, both as individuals and as the church.

—Lolly Dominski
Co-Pastor, Morton Grove Community Church
Adjunct Professor of Reformed Worship
McCormick Theological Seminary

Challenges for Today's Living: Studies in 1 Corinthians by William Powell Tuck follows in the impressive train of his nearly forty books by doing just what the title says: the volume calls on us to meet the challenges of modern life by heeding St. Paul's divine wisdom offered to folks in the troubled and troubling early church in Corinth. Dr. Tuck in turn guides us in our day in words that are practical, urgent, and totally relevant. As reader, you will come away a better person, and most certainly with a better understanding of this "favorite" of New Testament letters.

—J. Gordon Kingsley
Twelfth President of William Jewell College
Principal and Lecturer in British Studies
Harlaxton College, England

Smyth & Helwys Publishing, Inc.
6316 Peake Road
Macon, Georgia 31210-3960
1-800-747-3016
©2023 by William Powell Tuck
All rights reserved.

Chapter 11, "The Greatest of These Is Love," was originally published in *Love as a Way of Living* (Macon, GA: Smyth & Helwys Publishing, 2008).

Library of Congress Cataloging-in-Publication Data on file

WILLIAM POWELL TUCK

CHALLENGES
FOR
TODAY'S LIVING

STUDIES IN 1 CORINTHIANS

Also by William Powell Tuck

Lord, I Keep Getting a Busy Signal: Reaching for a Better Spiritual Connection

Overcoming Sermon Block: The Preacher's Workshop

A Revolutionary Gospel: Salvation in the Theology of Walter Rauschenbusch

Holidays, Holy Days, and Special Days

A Positive Word for Christian Lamenting: Funeral Homilies

The Forgotten Beatitude: Worshiping through Stewardship

Star Thrower: A Pastor's Handbook

A Pastoral Prophet: Sermons and Prayers of Wayne E. Oates (editor)

The Abiding Presence: Communion Meditations

Which Voice Will You Follow?

Beginning and Ending a Pastorate

The Difficult Sayings of Jesus

Conversations with My Grandchildren about God, Religion, and Life

The Rebirth of the Church

Markers Along the Way: The Signs of Jesus in the Gospel of John

Jesus' Journey to the Cross

Lessons from Old Testament Characters

Stories that Continue to Speak to Us Today: Looking Again at the Parables of Jesus

For Emily,
who understands and practices
Paul's teachings
in his love hymn
recounted in 1 Corinthians 13

Contents

Preface

For many Christian readers, 1 Corinthians is the favorite letter written by the Apostle Paul because of several special sections like the love chapter (13), the resurrection passage (15), the spiritual gifts segment (12), and others. Although there are deep and profound theological sections in this letter, it is without question Paul's most practical letter. Many of the sections are his personal response to particular questions members in the church have raised to him. Like many contemporary churches today, this early church had conflicts about pastoral leadership, the role of women in ministry, the appropriate manner to observe the Lord's Supper, the proper preaching in a congregation setting, and many others. Many of the challenges facing this young church are as relevant today as they were then. Paul's words to this first-century church at Corinth can still speak to the contemporary church's needs today.

Paul likely arrived in Corinth in the early fifties CE and found welcome in the home of two Jewish Christians, Aquila and Prisca, whose residence he used as a base to start the Corinthian church. One of the early converts was Crispus, the ruler of the local synagogue, and his family. Acts 18 gives a synopsis of the ministry of Paul in Corinth that lasted for a year and a half. After a rather sudden departure by Paul, likely due to controversy and crises, he did return several times to Corinth (2 Cor 12:14 and 13:1), one of these meetings being a "painful" visit cited in 2 Corinthians 2:1. Paul's First Epistle to the Corinthians was likely written from Ephesus and is filled with passion, gratitude, and concern. Paul's letter responds to at least ten areas of concern: church divisions, scandals, impurity, marriage, meats offered to idols, litigation in law courts, the behavior of women in worship, proper observance of the Lord's Supper, spiritual gifts, and the resurrection of the dead. Paul tried to respond in a concrete manner to the practical and ethical issues the young church had raised with him.

Scholars believe that Paul wrote five letters to the church at Corinth dealing with the situations that had arisen. We have two and maybe parts of three of these letters. Two of them are completely lost. The Second Epistle to the Corinthians probably contains two of the letters. The latter part of that epistle is probably the earlier letter (2 Cor 10–13), which is called the Severe Letter, and 2 Corinthians 1–9 is likely the later one. Another of the last letters may be contained in 2 Corinthians 6:14–7:1, but there is no way to know for certain. What we do know is that, through his letters, Paul tried to offer the Corinthians spiritual teaching and practical guidance.

As my focus for this book, I have selected several of his main themes and the way they may apply to our challenge to follow Christ today. My approach is to address these themes and seek to distill wisdom from them for the contemporary church. This book is not a commentary on 1 Corinthians but rather an attempt to follow the thematic approach Paul made with the Corinthians as I deal with issues raised by those who struggle with seeking to understand how one can serve Christ through the local church and in one's daily life. I want to express my appreciation to my friend and fellow minister, Rand Forder, for his careful proofreading of my original manuscript.

Chapter 1

The Gospel Addresses the City

1 Corinthians 1:1–3

Picture the city of Corinth in the Apostle Paul's day. It was a teeming metropolis—a commerce and trade center. It was a new city, a popular city, a wealthy city, and a city known for athletic events. The Isthmian Games were held there, and they were second only in importance to the Olympics in the ancient Greek world. Corinth had a stadium that seated 20,000 people, and there the people held their bloody gladiatorial events. Sometimes these gladiators would fight to the death with other men or with animals. They also had a more cultured theater that seated about 3,000. Here they had plays, music, boxing, and wrestling.

The city was noted as well for its religion, with temples to Apollos, Zeus, Dionysus, Isis, and many others. There were two temples to the goddess of love. Priestesses of the goddess of common love, Aphrodite, would descend from Acropolis at night to sell themselves on the streets as sacred prostitutes. To a sailor, the mention of a Corinthian woman was almost synonymous with speaking about a prostitute. Corinth was identified with wealth, pleasure, and immorality. It was a city renowned for loose living and a city where tradition said only the wealthy could afford to live.

This is the city to which Paul wrote his epistle, 1 Corinthians. He was probably living there when he wrote these words to Rome:

Thus, because they have not seen fit to acknowledge God, he has given them up to their own depraved reason. This leads them to break all rules of conduct. They are filled with every kind of injustice, mischief, rapacity, and malice; they are one mass of envy, murder, rivalry, treachery, and malevolence; whisperers and scandal-mongers, hateful to God, insolent, arrogant, and boastful; they invent new kinds of mischief, they show no loyalty to parents, no conscience, no fidelity to their plighted word; they are without natural affection and without pity. They know well enough the just decree of God, that those who behave like this deserve to die, and yet they do it; not only so, they actually applaud such practices. (Rom 1:28-32, New English Bible)

You name it and Paul seemed to use it as an adjective to describe those who lived in Corinth and how far from God they were in their living. In some ways, unfortunately, the church at Corinth reflected too much the society in which it existed. Paul addressed the issues of divisions and quarrels within the church, immorality within the church, secularism within the church, their distorted worship habits, and also their misunderstanding of death and the resurrection. Sometimes people say too quickly and without enough knowledge, "We need to be like the New Testament church." If you want to be like a New Testament church, for heaven's sake, don't be like the church at Corinth. It was one of the most corrupt, immoral, and divided churches one could find. Unfortunately, too many have used that as a model of what the church should be like today!

The Gospel Message Addresses Cities

One of the concepts we have of the gospel today is that it often is shared primarily using rural, pastoral images. This is one of the difficulties the modern church confronts when it tries to speak to people who live in urban settings. We forget that the Apostle Paul wrote letters to Rome, Corinth, Ephesus, Philippi, Colossae, Thessalonica, and Galatia. He wrote letters to the churches of his day that were located in big cities.

Jesus himself approached Jerusalem and wept over the city: "Oh Jerusalem, Jerusalem," he cried (Luke 19). Why did he weep? Well, he may have wept because the city that was supposed to be the holy city was not holy at all. It was a city filled with sinners. Maybe he wept because of the distortion of holiness that had taken place in that city. Maybe he wept because the one who had come as God Immanuel had been rejected by the city. The city that had sung "Lift up your gates and let the king of glory come in" would reject the King of Glory when he came in.

I wonder if Jesus Christ today does not weep over his "Jerusalems." Does he not continue to weep over Chicago, New York, Boston, Washington, Richmond, Louisville, and cities across the world? I wonder if he does not weep over the cities because of what has happened there and often because the gospel he has given to us does not address the cities.

Many people love cities. They love the skyscrapers. They love the big stores and shopping malls. They love the bustling crowds, the lights in the windows, the restaurants, the theaters, and the entertainment opportunities. They even love to drive on its various expressways in the snarl of traffic. Some people love the hustle and bustle of big cities. But some folks don't. They don't like the odor, noise, pollution, and crowds. The endless flow of traffic makes them nervous. They do not know how to live comfortably in big cities. These people do not really love the city; they desert it on the weekends. Their hearts are not there because they flee to the farm, the lake, the mountains, or the country. They flee to get away from the city.

But the city is where many of us live today. "The city is more important than ever," Stephen Um and Justin Buzzard argue. "Right now, more people live in cities than at any other time in human history. Never before has the majority of the world's population been in urban populations."[1] The gospel must address the city where we live. Before 1900 in our country, 60 percent of people lived on farms. Today more than 85 percent of people live in cities—in urban settings. If the gospel of Jesus Christ does not address the world where we live in the cities, then it will miss its greatest opportunity today.

The Voice of Cities

Listen. Cities have voices, and you can hear them. You can hear the rumbling of buses, taxis, trucks, and cars as they go up and down the streets. You can hear the murmurs of sadness, depression, fatigue, and hopelessness. You can hear the cries of pain, agony, and frustration. You can hear the shouts of violence, crime, and unemployment. You can hear the whispers of loneliness, isolation, alienation, greed, hate, lust, and fear. You can hear the songs of pleasure, entertainment, delight, and joy. You can hear the hum of factories, businesses, schools, and hospitals. Cities have all kinds of voices that come to us demanding time and attention.

The city today, I believe, will determine what our civilization will be like. It is the heart of today's civilization. The direction it takes will affect the state and nation. In the world today, one finds that the major universities, hospitals, and law schools are located in or near cities. Cities often determine our entertainment, art, drama, architecture, concerts, newspapers, and other cultural values. Most business or industry is located in or near cities. Much of our lifestyle is determined by cities, and if the gospel does not address the cities, it will not reach people for God in a meaningful way today. The theme I am seeking to advocate is that *the gospel of Jesus Christ addresses cities in a powerful way with good news.* The gospel is meaningful to those of us who live in cities today. The Christian message is not just a word for people who live in country atmospheres. Too quickly and too easily, many have dismissed the gospel by saying that it was written in a time when there were not many big cities, so it could not have anything to say to people in cities. Sometimes the teachings of Jesus are depicted as being so steeped in rural images that people do not see how they could have anything to do with the modern world.

Established in a Quest for Security

I would like to make some suggestions regarding this problem. One is that we need to remember that cities were established originally in a quest for security. In ancient Egyptian hieroglyphics, the earliest known symbol for the city was an ideogram. The figure depicted a circle with a cross inside of it. The cross represented the interchanges like roads, canals, and other thoroughfares within the cities. The circle represented security. People secured themselves with moats or walls to prevent invaders from coming into their territory. For centuries people have gathered in cities for reasons of security and protection. To live by oneself only with one's family was much more dangerous, and an enemy could come down from the hills or from nearby and attack them. Farmers soon realized that they needed each other's protection from common enemies. In small towns people are able to respond when the fire alarm sounds, and everybody leaves his job and goes rushing to put out the fire. Voluntary fire departments are not the answer to fire prevention in a large city. Trained, experienced, paid people need to be available to meet the immediate needs of those who live in a large city. People still gather together for reasons of security.

In the book of Genesis (Gen 3:16ff), we read that Cain was the first builder of a city. After he had slain his brother, Abel, he went to the land of Nod, which in Hebrew means the land of wandering. From his days of wandering, he desired a more permanent place, so he got married and built a city. He named the city he built Enoch, which means *imitation*. The word "city" in Hebrew means *terror*, *watchful angel*, or *vigilance*. The city became the place that symbolized security for those who wanted to stop wandering and to have the protection of other people.

Strangers Gathered in Cities

Cities were also a place where strangers could gather together. Cities are composed of people who originally came from many countries and backgrounds. They are strangers whose background is often unknown, and they hope to get lost in the crowd. They put up "private" and "keep out" signs. "Icy conditions are ahead" when one tries to relate to them. The Scriptures refer to these folks as aliens. Even in our own day, we speak about the immigrants who come to our country from another nation who must register here because they are foreigners from another culture.

We know about strangers. We tell our children, "Don't accept rides from strangers." "Don't take candy from strangers." "Don't talk to strangers." A bank will seldom cash checks from strangers. We are all cautious about people we do not know. We might knock at the door of someone we do not know, and we may be met by a most pleasant person. But there is no way we can determine what goes on behind those doors, or in the attic, or in the basement, or in the other rooms of the house. If that person is a stranger to us, there may be many things hidden within that house or buried deep within that individual. Paul wrote to the church at Ephesus, "Thus, you are no longer strangers (aliens) in a foreign land but fellow citizens with God's people, members of God's household" (Eph 2:19). Those within the church are no longer strangers. We are bound together in fellowship with Christ and each other.

City Ghettos

Cities also are made up of various kinds of ghettos. Some of the ghettos consist of slums, but there are also velvet ghettos. There is a child's saying that goes:

> Hark, Hark, the dogs do bark,
> The beggars are coming to town.
> Some in rags,
> and some in tags,
> And some in velvet gowns.

There are beggars of all kinds in the world. Some of them in our town are in rags, and they need help. There are also some with all kinds of tags around them for identification. But there are also beggars who wear velvet gowns.

These people may think of themselves as self-made and secure. Sometimes they are leaders in the community, but they struggle with problems of loneliness, alienation, alcoholism, and more. Their problems may be on a different level than those of people in the slums, but they have problems. A friend of mine was struggling between two churches that were interested in calling him as pastor. One was a large church on the West Coast. The other was a much smaller church in a smaller town, but its membership was mostly affluent people. He didn't know whether to go there or not because he wasn't sure if going to a wealthy congregation as pastor would be a compromise for him. One of the committee members said to him, "Look, we are sinners, too. And we have all kinds of problems and need someone to help us with them." The cities are made up of all kinds of individuals; some can be beggars in velvet as well as beggars in slum ghettos. The gospel needs to address these people as well.

Some People Are Seen Only for Their Functions

The city too often sees people only for their functions. We see people as bankers, lawyers, or carpenters. We see them as maids, taxi drivers, or bus drivers. We see them as accountants, teachers, ministers, or businesspeople. We never see them as individuals because we never get beyond their contact as someone who waits on our table, drives the bus or taxi we ride, helps us in the store, or does business with us. We do not see them as authentic human beings apart from their functions.

One of our church members recently asked another as he came to worship, "Is it okay with you if I'm me today?" That person replied, "What do you mean?" "I'm just asking you today," the other continued with a wink in his eye, "if it's okay if I be myself today?" Too often we do not really let other people be themselves. We want to categorize them in terms of their functions. When we do that, they cannot be authentic human beings but are confined to what *we* envision them to be by the roles we see them play. The role and the person become one.

Living without a Past

Our cities can also be places where people seek to live without a past. We meet strangers. We do not know them, and they do not know us. Sometimes no inquiry is made as to where they have come from or what they have done; they are simply here. Some of them, of course, do not want us to know. They want to begin where they are in this moment. The past is past, and they want to begin in the present. Helmut Thielicke, a German theologian, tells the story of a German play titled *Traveler without Luggage*.[2] In this play, a young soldier has been severely wounded in battle, and he has lost all memory of his past. Except for his loss of memory, he is okay. His memory of the past, however, is completely gone. The military advertises in the papers and over the radio to see if they can find anyone who can identify this young man. A family finally recognizes him as their son. They know that he is their son. They talk to him about things from the past, but in no way is his memory jogged. He simply cannot recall them. One day, a maid who had cared for him as an infant tells him about a birthmark on a certain place on his body. She knows this because she had bathed him when he was a baby. He gets a mirror and looks at the spot on his body, and sure enough, it is true. But it is not enough for him. He now knows that he belonged to this family, but he still doesn't know them. Another family asks him to come and talk with them. They know immediately that he is not their son, and he knows now that they cannot be his parents, but he decides to go ahead and be their son and their heir because he can start off without a past and just be who he wants to be in this moment.

In the city, a lot of people want to do what this man in the play does. Some want to sever their memory of the past because it's not good or because it has been troublesome or difficult. The city for many becomes an opportunity to get lost in the teeming multitude. Many want to become lost in the mob.

Addressed as God's Church

Does the gospel say anything to those of us who try to live in the city? Paul says several helpful things in this brief passage. The first is this: He addresses this letter to the church of God in Corinth. It is not written to the church of Corinth. It is written to the church of *God*. In every city, if the church is to make any vital difference, it must never be just "our" church. It must be God's church. It must be the church of the living God. It must be the church that challenges and addresses the city to rise to the standard God wants it to have and not be content with what it has already achieved. In every city, political decisions are often made that slowly close off the inner city, and it begins to die. People move out into the suburbs and create small cities there. These small cities do not really support the larger city because they have become separate cities, and the larger city slowly becomes depressed. We also build expressways so that the people who live in suburban areas can come in to work in the inner city, and that, of course, adds to the depression because they usually do not support the city with their taxes.

If you and I are a part of a city, we know that the inner city needs the gospel of Christ, and we are challenged by its needs. For the poor, hungry, and needy, we must continuously be on the move with the good news of Christ to address the needs of these people. The voice of Christ should be heard where people are living in the inner city. Through our efforts, we are to let them know that the presence of the church of God is there.

The Message Needs to Be Understood

We, like Paul, also need to let the church of God translate God's message to the city where it is being proclaimed in terms that the city can understand. When Paul spoke to the Gentile churches, he did not use the country images of Palestine. He used legal, philosophical, and urban terminology that they would understand when he talked about the good news of Christ. He translated the gospel so that the urban people of his day could hear its message. One of the problems in our modern cities is that too many people want the city churches to be nothing but reflections of the country churches where they used to go. They want us to stay in the country dress, the country style, and do not want the city churches to address the urban needs of people today. I know of a Southern Baptist church in New York City that tried to remain like a small country church, and it died. And well it should have! It never attempted to address the needs of the people around it in language that they could understand. The gospel needs to be translated continuously so it addresses people where they are and serves their needs in this moment, in the city.

A number of years ago, James Conn was visiting Atlanta, Georgia. One night, when he was looking through the yellow pages for a restaurant, he came across one listed under the title "The Church of God Grill." He decided to call them and see what kind of food they served. In the course of his conversation, he asked, "How did you happen to get the name 'The Church of God Grill'?" The man answered, "Well, we started a mission downtown and we began selling chicken after the service. Then the chicken business started getting so good that we started cutting back on the church service. And the chicken business continued to get even better, so finally we cut out having the church services altogether and just sold chicken. But we kept the name 'Church of God Grill.'"[3]

Do I have to spell out an interpretation of that story? Too often that is symbolic of what has happened to the church of Christ today. Some churches are so enamored with their programs, as worthy as these may be, that they end up doing nothing but focusing on the goods they are selling. We have become the Church of God Grill and have forgotten to share the good news of the gospel of Jesus Christ with the world. The Christian church is always the church of God and not merely the programs we promote or sponsor. The power of God's spirit works through God's church to address the world today.

Consecrated in Christ

Notice further that Paul says this epistle is written to those who are sanctified or consecrated in Christ. The church of God is made up of those who have been redeemed by the power of Christ. It is composed of those who have been set apart because of an experience with Jesus Christ. He is our Savior. We are consecrated by his death. "Grace to you and peace," Paul said. The faithful acknowledged that Christ was "their Lord and ours." God's word comes into our world to address those who are fragmented and torn, distorted and twisted by sin, with the good news of God's grace in Jesus Christ.

A six-year-old was sitting and listening as his parents talked to friends one night. They were all discussing their various ailments. Right before the boy went to bed, one of the people said to another, "Well, I guess it could best be summed up by saying, 'Everything just seems to be going to pieces.'" That night as the little boy went to say his prayers, he said, "God, bless Daddy and Mommy and all those other people who are falling apart."

To some extent, we are all falling apart in one way or another. There are pieces of our lives that we feel have pulled us in different directions, and we need the power of God to address us as people in this day and age with a sense of the wholeness that comes from Christ, who pulls us together. The word *salvation* means "whole," "full," or "complete." God, then, pulls us together and makes us whole, full, complete people in this day and age.

Allen Walker, who was a minister in Sydney, Australia, had a service in his church called "The Life Line." This was a telephone answering service for people who were contemplating suicide. It was staffed twenty-four hours a day. One Saturday night he received a call from a man who told him he was getting ready to commit suicide. Dr. Walker talked to the man and encouraged him not to take his life and asked him to come the next day to the service where he was speaking on "Life's Glorious Failures." The man came to the service and later talked by telephone again with Dr. Walker and indicated that his sermon had helped. They set up an appointment to meet later. Before Dr. Walker could talk with the man, however, he received word that the man had committed suicide. The dejected man had turned on the unlit gas in his room and was later found dead. Walker went to the man's room and was handed a note that the man had addressed to him. It read, "I am afraid my faith has failed me. Please pray for me. I am not worth saving. I am a failure. I am leaving the world unwanted, unloved, and without hope."[4] This man died in a city with two million people.

There are people all over the city who feel unwanted, unloved, and without hope. There are thousands of people in the city with real hurts and needs, and hundreds in the church are called to reach out to them with the good news of Jesus Christ. If you feel that you are only a function and have been depersonalized, or that nobody really cares for you and you remain a stranger in a large city, hear the word from Jesus Christ telling you that you are his child—a son, a daughter—and that he loves you and cares for you. To those who feel fragmented, twisted, and alienated, Christ brings wholeness. He assures us that we can become God's children and be made one in him. To those who feel that life is helpless and hopeless, Christ gives purpose, hope, and meaning. To those who are lost, he gives place. To the weary, he gives strength. To the sinful, he gives forgiveness. To the anxious, he gives peace.

The Saints in Our Churches

Finally, Paul tells us that we are to be "saints." This epistle is addressed to the "saints in Corinth." I know we don't like the word "saint" much today. If someone were to ask you if you were a saint, most likely you would say, "Not me, I'm not a saint." But in fifteen of the twenty-seven New Testament books, Christians are called saints. "Saint" means those who are set apart. You and I, as Christians, are set apart and consecrated to be like Christ. The people who were to make a difference in the city of Corinth were the Christians. They were the saints there. You are to go into your city of New York, Washington D.C., Louisville, Richmond, or wherever you live, and be the saint in your office, school, shop, marketplace, business—wherever you are. You and I are to be the saints for Christ in this city who live out the gospel of Jesus Christ in our lives. You and I are called to be set apart for Christ's service by the power of his love and grace. We are called to be saints. You and I are the salt, the light, and the leaven in the world, and if we do not go into the world and God is not able to use us, then God's message becomes distorted, dim, and twisted because of the image that comes through us.

When the writer of the book of Revelation came to his final image for what life beyond this one would be like, he did not use the figure of a home or a church but the figure of a city—New Jerusalem. Abraham went forth looking for a city whose builder and maker was God. God has made for us a city in eternity where you and I can be brothers and sisters. In that city, there are no bosses or employers. All are working together in one family, one race, and one city because we are God's children.

God loves the city because God loves people. God expects you and me to be the saints in the city and to make a difference in the lives of those who live there. Those who are torn, fragmented, twisted, strangers, and depersonalized because of the city need to hear the voice of Christ as he addresses the city's voice, hears its cry, and speaks to its needs. May we hear the gospel of Christ as it addresses our city, but most important of all may we hear it as it addresses your needs and mine.

Chapter 2

Remembering to Be Thankful

1 Corinthians 1:4-9

Several years ago, I read and kept an article from the Louisville newspaper that Erma Bombeck wrote about the "Miss Manners" column. She said, "I don't know Miss Manners personally, but she is a voice in the wilderness, crying out to an audience who can't hear her because they've never been taught to be quiet while someone else is talking. Courtesy and civility have become as obsolete in our society as carbon paper and coal."

Then she went on to write about our lack of good manners and the unwillingness of many to say, "Thank you." She continued,

> I haven't finished with my kids yet. They still need work. It's an ongoing challenge. I'm still teaching manners. I used to have nightmares that, as my son was receiving the Nobel Prize for literature, I would crawl onto the stage on my hands and knees and tug at his pant leg and whisper, "Now, what do you say to the nice man?" and he would say, "Oh, yea, thanks."[1]

My parents had to teach me to say "Thank you," just as I had to teach my own children. We do not automatically express appreciation. It has to be learned.

The First Thanksgiving

The first Thanksgiving celebration in what became the United States of America was observed in 1619 at the Berkeley Plantation, located on the James River between Williamsburg and Richmond, Virginia. In 1623, William Bradford signed the proclamation that established the "first" official Thanksgiving in our country. But it had been observed for four years before this official declaration. It was not an easy time for those early pilgrims. We have all read about the hardships they underwent. Many of the pilgrims lost their lives, and from our perspective, the remaining few had very little for which to be grateful. But a Native people, the Wampanoag, shared their land, food, and knowledge of the environment with the English, and with their help, the English had the successful harvest that led to the First Thanksgiving in 1623 where they expressed their thanksgiving to God for their lives and the small victory they had won in this new land. It seems strange that 400 years later, with an abundance of blessings, many of us suffer from voice fatigue when it comes to expressing thanksgiving. We simply take our blessings for granted. We somehow assume that all we have has always been and always will be. So we do not really bother with expressing gratitude to anyone.

Ingratitude Is Too Common

Unfortunately, ingratitude almost seems to be a part of our culture today. It has deep roots. Some years ago, off Lake Michigan on a freezing winter day, a ship sank near Evanston, Illinois. Some students from Northwestern University swam through the cold water to rescue the people who were drowning. One young man rescued seventeen people. He swam back and forth repeatedly through the icy water until they were all safe. He spent so much time in the freezing water that he came down with an incurable illness that left him disabled for life. When someone was talking to this young man later, they asked him if he regretted what he had done. He said he did not regret it; he thought he had done the best he could under the circumstances. But the one thing that he could not understand was this: of the seventeen people whose lives he saved that day, not a single one of them ever came to see him. None ever wrote him a "thank you" note, expressed appreciation in any way at all, or offered any help to him during his illness—not a single one.

The Difficulty of Expressing Thanks

Too often we simply accept what is done for us without verbalizing any kind of expression of appreciation. Others are simply supposed to do those things for us because that is their job. They are parents; they are teachers; they are merely fulfilling their functions. We take so much for granted. Many never expect to express appreciation, but they can certainly express complaints if everything is not just right or they do not get their way. Complaints and gripes quickly rush to our mouths to be expressed.

A man had worked hard at his job. He had a job where he had to stand on his feet all day. He got on the bus to go home one afternoon and felt weary and tired. The bus was crowded but he found a seat. An older woman got on later, and he got up and gave her his seat. After she sat down, he looked at her and said, "Beg your pardon, did you say something?" She replied, "No, I didn't say anything." He said, "Oh, I thought you said 'thank you.' Excuse me." Isn't it amazing how difficult it is for the words "thank you" to come to our lips, whereas complaints often come rushing forward?

Thanksgiving is a distinctive American holiday, and I guess it is good that we set aside one day to remind us to be thankful, because if we didn't have that one day, I wonder when some of us would ever get around to expressing thanksgiving. Any time we use the word "holiday," it should remind us of its derivation, which is "holy day." Thanksgiving should be a reminder to us that every day ought to be a day of thanksgiving. The word "thanks" is rooted in *think*. When we are thoughtful, we give thanks.

The Psalms Are Filled with Thanksgivings

The Psalms are filled with expressions of gratitude to God. The psalmists call us to a room called "Remember." "Enter his gates with thanksgiving" (100:4). "I give you thanks, O Lord, with my whole heart" (138:1). "O give thanks to the Lord, for he is good" (118:1). "Bless the Lord, O my soul, and forget not all his benefits"(103:2). The psalmists were constantly praising God for his bounty and blessings.

Paul's Appeal for Thankfulness

The Apostle Paul wrote to the Corinthian church and expressed his thanksgiving to God for them and for the gifts God had given them. Paul opened with a word of thankfulness. He did this in other letters but not in Galatians. He had no thankfulness for them, likely because some of the people in the church at Galatia did not believe Paul was a real apostle, and, therefore, they should not listen to what he said. But he offers only faint praise for the Corinthians (2 Cor 6:14–7:1). His basis of thanksgiving is what God has done in Christ. The Corinthians had few material gifts but had the gift of speech. In other letters, Paul had praised the churches for their faith, hope, and love. But the Corinthians were not known for their love of each other or their support of Paul. The church was filled with quarreling and strife.

Our Personal Challenge for Thankfulness

I want to challenge you today to express your thankfulness. Saying thanks is only a small part of giving thanks. Thankfulness is more than manners; it is an expression of our moral character. Begin today by giving thanks to God for the gift of life. You and I had nothing to do with our own existence. It is a gift from our parents and ultimately from God. Life, your life and mine, is a gift to be treasured and spent wisely.

Several years ago, my wife, Emily, and I had lunch with some friends from another state. While we were eating, my friend, who celebrates the same birth month as mine, asked me what I did when I turned forty. Before I could answer, he said, "I cried." Laughing, I said, "Being a minister and conducting so many funerals, I was just glad to be alive!" To be alive is a great gift we ought to celebrate. I challenge you to be thankful.

It is easy, it seems, to receive so much and still have a difficult time expressing gratitude. We take many things for granted. When was the last time you expressed thanks to God because you can think? It has not been too recently, I expect. We simply take the fact that we can think, that we can solve problems, that we can look at something and arrive at a solution, for granted. But I know a middle-aged attorney who developed a disease that slowly took away his ability to recall information, and he had to give up his practice. He had one of the finest practices in the city, but he could no longer remember where he was. His physical body was perfectly healthy, but his mind was slowly going. When he would go to the Y to exercise, he might see you and know that he was supposed to know you, but he could not recall your name. He might say hello to you and then in a moment speak to you again because he could no longer remember who you were or that he had already spoken to you. When was the last time you thanked God for your ability to think?

When was the last time you thanked God that you can see? We take our sight for granted. My father, who several years ago had cataract surgery and a lens implant, reminded me of the difficulty he had in seeing. We take our eyes for granted until we cannot see.

When was the last time you expressed thanksgiving for your hearing? Several years ago, I lost partial hearing in one of my ears. Thankfully, I regained my hearing in that ear several weeks later. Since that time, I have always been much more appreciative and understanding of people who have difficulty in hearing.

When was the last time you thanked God that your body functions properly? I remember visiting a patient in the hospital who complained to me about a problem they were having with a bodily function.

We take all these of these things for granted and rarely express thanksgiving to God for them. We just assume that everything will always work until it no longer does. We take for granted the food on our tables, the clothes we wear, the house we live in, and the job we have. When was the last time you thanked God for your parents, your children, your spouse, your friends? We take them for granted until we can no longer express our thanksgiving for them because they are no longer with us. Death or distance may have removed them from us. As I am writing these lines, I received an email alerting me to the death of a close friend in another state. I can no longer talk with or consult him.

Have you ever thanked God for the person who first led you into your spiritual awareness of God? Have you expressed thanks for the person who introduced you to God and to Jesus Christ? Have you expressed thanks for those who taught you about right and wrong and guided you to seek high moral values in life? Have you ever paused to thank God for your parents, Sunday school teachers, ministers, grandparents, or whoever were the first ones to lead you to God?

An old legend states that God once sent two angels down to earth. One was to gather a basket filled with petitions—all the requests that people were asking of God. The other angel was to collect a basket filled with thanksgivings from the people. The angel who returned with the basket of requests could hardly carry it because it was so heavy. But the one with the basket of thanksgiving expressions hardly had any notes at all. Why is it so difficult for us to give thanks to God for the great bounty that we have?

Paul Admonishes Christians to Be Thankful

In writing to the Thessalonians, Paul admonished, "In all things give thanks to God" (1 Thess 5:18). Paul must have had an easy life to write such words. Right? Wrong. Paul had a difficult time. For preaching about Christ, he was beaten, stoned, shipwrecked, imprisoned, and run out of town. Even some people in the church found him too serious, especially the Corinthians. They wanted frivolity and immorality in their church. Others thought Paul's writings and preaching were heavy and difficult to understand. But he challenged them to think deeply in the faith and take up their cross and follow Christ. He had experienced rejection, failure, and dark times, but he knew how to rejoice in good and bad times. He knew that God was working in all things to bring about God's will (Rom 8:28).

Paul didn't say give thanks *for* all things but *in* all things. Thanksgiving is not reserved just for the good times. Paul urges us to learn the difficult lesson of expressing thanksgiving in the midst of the bad times as well as in the good times. A vital faith makes us want to lift up our voices in praise: "Now thank we all our God." We need to learn to praise God on dark, rainy days as well as on bright, sunny days. We need to learn to praise God on days of discouragement as well as in times when we are on the mountaintops filled with enthu-siasm. We need to learn to express praise to God in times of illness as well as in times of health. We need to learn to express thanksgiving to God in times of death as well as in times of life. We exclaim with Job, "The LORD giveth and the LORD taketh away. Blessed be the name of the LORD" (Job 1:21). We can learn to verbalize praise in all things when we know that nothing can separate us from the presence of God. Whether times are good or bad, God is still present with us to sustain us in everything that happens.

Israel learned some of its greatest lessons about God in the wilder-ness (see Numbers 14; Deut 8:2, 16, 29:5; Neh 9:21; Josh 5:6). Paul had suffered greatly for God through persecution, imprisonment, and rejection. But in the midst of all his suffering, he could still say, "In all things, give thanks unto God."

Thankfulness Requires Effort

I am not convinced that we simply become a thankful people without working at it. Thankfulness takes effort. It should be cultivated in our lives and taught to our children and others. We begin by trying to teach our children to learn to be thankful for the small things of life. We teach them to be thankful for their clothes, food, home, parents, and church. They should be taught to verbalize and express thank-fulness to others for the things they receive—gifts, food, education, toys, etc. Another step in learning thankfulness is to express thanks to God. We learn to express our thanks at mealtime as we praise God for the bounty we have—large or small. We remind our children that all gifts ultimately come to us from the hand of a loving God.

When we learn to be thankful, it enables us to remember, and when we remember what others have done for us—parents, teachers, and friends—then we remember to be more grateful. When we are more grateful, we are able to express our gratitude more realistically because we remember. We remember that many of our blessings are not really of our own doing but are the result of what others have done for us through their time, effort, energy, love, and devotion. Everything has not come to us simply by our own strength. As we remember, it also makes us humbler because we realize that none of us is totally self-made. We can never be selfish because we have received so much from others in life, and we express our gratitude to God for them. Having received so much from others, we acknowledge our indebtedness to them and express our gratitude for them and the great blessings they have shared with us. Most of all we praise God for God's great blessings to us.

Let us cultivate gratitude. Work at it. Drop notes to others and express your thankfulness. Let us remind our children not to take for granted what we have and are. When is the last time you thanked your wife for the many things she does for you? Too often we take them for granted. When is the last time you expressed appreciation to your wife and didn't just assume that she knew it? Or, when was the last time you verbalized appreciation to your husband or said "I love you"? Children, when have you last expressed your love and appreciation for your parents, and parents, when have you last done the same for your children? Singles, when did you express appreciation for friends or family? We take each other for granted too often.

One Thanksgiving, a man was talking to a group of friends about what he was thankful for. One of the things he mentioned was a schoolteacher who taught him thirty years ago. He said this teacher taught him to love English literature, and his love for reading had helped change his life and enriched it with meaning. His friend asked him, "Have you ever written this lady and told her that?" "No, I never have," he said. "Why don't you do it?" his friend asked. "Take a few moments and write her a note." So he did. He wrote a letter to Miss Wendt, his high school English teacher. The letter traveled from one address to another until it finally reached Miss Wendt. She was living in a small one-room apartment. She sat down that very day and wrote a note back. "Dear Willie," she wrote, "I can't tell you how much your note meant to me. I am in my eighties, living alone in a small room, cooking my own meals, lonely and, like the last leaf of fall, lingering behind. You will be interested to know that I taught school for fifty years and yours is the first note of appreciation I ever received. It came on a blue, cold morning and it cheered me as nothing has for years."

When was the last time you took a moment to express appreciation to somebody who meant a great deal to you? I challenge *you* this week to drop a note of thanksgiving to somebody—a teacher, a friend, a relative who has enriched your life. You can never imagine what it may mean to them. After all, you do know what it means to receive such a note. Think what it might mean to someone if you took the time to address a note to them and say, "What you did for me when I was young or down was helpful. I want you to know it." If not a note, express a word of appreciation verbally to your spouse, child, or parent. Let us express our thanksgiving unto God and learn to do so "in all things."

Chapter 3

Quarrels in the Church
1 Corinthians 1:10-18

A number of years ago, a minister retired who was noted for a particular controversy that had occurred in his church. It was a controversy about the side of the church where the piano should be located—left or right. The church had actually split over that issue. The pastor had been rather forceful in his opinion on which side he thought it should be placed. Later he served as pastor of the church that split off from the mother church. After his retirement, he told a younger pastor, "You know, I consider that experience the high mark in my ministry. The stand I took in that particular church was a significant time in my life." The other minister remarked, "That is really interesting. By the way, on which side of the church did you think the piano should be placed?" The retired preacher said, "Why, I thought it should go . . . no, it was . . . Elsie, which side of the church did I think the piano should be placed on?"

When you get down to it, many controversies in churches are probably just that trite. At times they have been very divisive. The Apostle Paul was no stranger to quarrels in the church, especially in the Corinthian church. He was in Ephesus and had received a word from Chloe, a woman in the church at Corinth, about the divisions in the faith community. Most scholars believe that Chloe was probably a wealthy merchant in the church. Paul had received word from her people—probably her slaves who were carrying some goods and messages for her to Ephesus from Corinth—that there had been quarrels in the church in Corinth.

The Greek word used here for *quarrels* literally means "battle-strife," "contentions," or "rivalry." It was a serious problem. The word indicates that there was literally "a tear in the fabric" of the church itself. Paul felt that he had to write to them and discuss this serious problem. He believed that the most distinctive mark of the church was its unity in Christ. In the twelfth chapter of his Epistle to the Corinthians, he goes to great lengths to discuss the importance of unity in Christ.

Divisions in the Corinthian Church

In the church at Corinth, different divisions and rival groups had set themselves up in parties within the congregation, and they even had particular slogans. One of them said, "I belong to Paul." This group was composed of the charter members of the Corinthian church. They had responded to Paul's message and had been converted under his leadership. These were the Gentile Christians in the church, who were likely the more liberal element. Another party slogan was "I belong to Apollos." Apollos was a noted Alexandrian preacher. He had come to Corinth likely on one of his preaching missions, and the people had been left spellbound by his preaching gifts. Acts 18 makes note of his great gifts of preaching and his vast knowledge of the Scriptures. The Corinthians had never heard a preacher that profound and powerful. Coming from Alexandria, he probably was also a part of the group that gave intelligent understanding to the Christian faith. He surely attracted to the faith the more highly intelligent people in the community. They belonged to Apollos because he had made the faith more understandable.

Another group in the church claimed allegiance to Cephas. Cephas was the Aramaic name for Peter. Some have speculated that Simon Peter may have come to Corinth at some point and led some to Christ, though there is no evidence of that. More likely, some Christians from Palestine, who had come under the influence of Peter and been converted by him, later moved to Corinth. This group probably represented the more orthodox or rigid group within the church.

Finally, there was the party that said, "I belong to Christ." This was the group that may have been converted by James the brother of Jesus. They may have claimed a more direct line to God. They were

Gnostics who claimed to have superior wisdom over other Christians. They didn't belong to the minor groups. They believed they had a special revelation from God and belonged solely to Christ above all others. But in this kind of thinking, Christ was just another party tag for them.

These particular quarrels were setting one church member against another to the point that the whole church was being literally torn apart. Paul challenged them and asked, "Is Christ divided?" If Christ is to be the head, then there is a united body. Christ cannot be the head if there is no body. If the church is torn and fragmented, Paul is saying that there really is no church in existence, because Christ is not the Lord of division. The most distinctive note of the Christian community is its unity (1 Cor 12:12-27). Fragmentation and division in the body were very serious to Paul, and he felt that they had to be confronted. He wrote to the Corinthian church from Ephesus. He had founded the church at Corinth, spent several years there, and was deeply distressed by what had happened.

Paul himself had become the center of some of the controversy. People had said insulting things about him. They had criticized his appearance and speech. They didn't like his crude speech because it was not as polished as the pure Greek dialect, so they made fun of it. They misquoted him, misrepresented him, misunderstood him, and lied about what he had said. Paul was deeply hurt by this. He did not know exactly what to do. He wrote five letters to them, as I indicated in the introduction. The letters to the church were then carried by a messenger aboard a ship. It probably took days, weeks, or months to get the message to its location, and then it took days and months to get the response back.

Disturbed by the Divisions

Paul was deeply disturbed by what had happened. In this first chapter he refers to the Corinthians twice as "my brothers and sisters." This was not a taskmaster seeking to rebuke them but one who loved them deeply. The term "brothers and sisters" should have indicated to them that Paul wanted to embrace them and draw them back into the unity of the church family. Division was a serious problem for

Paul. He believed that divisiveness indicated that these people were not really converted in the first place. Paul states that divisiveness in the church is a sign of the fleshly nature, and the "sign of the flesh" is clearly an indication to Paul of an unconverted state. Divisiveness in the church, Paul is saying, is a sign that some may think they are Christian, but they really are not because they have not let the power of Christ penetrate their very being. They are still living "after the flesh," as an unconverted person (3:1-3). Quarreling was to Paul a clear sign that a person was without Christ as Lord. He refers to this in 2 Corinthians 2:30, Romans 1:29, and Galatians 5:20.

In the Epistle to Titus we read these words:

> Avoid foolish controversies and genealogies and arguments and quarrels about the law because they are unprofitable and useless. Warn a divisive person once and then warn him a second time. After that have nothing to do with him. You may be sure that such a man is warped and sinful and is self-condemned. (3:9)

Paul did not have much patience with those who continued to create divisiveness within the church, and he labeled them clearly as being those apart from Christ and belonging to the unspiritual fleshly nature.

Baptists and Divisiveness

Baptists have not always dealt kindly with those who caused divisiveness within the church. The oldest Baptist fellowship in this country, the Charleston Association, founded in 1775, spells out vividly in its *Baptist Church Discipline* how the church should deal with those within the fellowship who cause divisiveness. There are three steps in this process: *First,* they rebuked such people. If they did not respond to rebuke, then the *second step* was to censure them and suspend them from the church for a period of time until they confessed and changed from their divisive ways. The *third step* was excommunication. They were put out of the church if they would not change. This is from the oldest Baptist tradition.[1] It reaches back to the New Testament in its understanding of the seriousness of divisiveness within the body of Christ. Divisiveness is far from the spirit of Christ.

Factors Causing Division in the Church

There were three factors that seemed to cause quarrels and divisiveness in the early church. The *first* was that some people believed they had superior wisdom over other Christians. They thought they had special insight into the mind of Christ, and they looked upon others as not quite as good as they were at being Christians. Paul wiped all of that aside with one sweeping blow when he said that all human wisdom, compared to God's wisdom, is foolishness. Paul affirmed that it was by the foolishness of the cross that we understand the power of God's spirit.

Second, there were also people who were guilty of the sin of pride. They caused divisiveness in the church because of their pridefulness. They boasted that their party was the right one—the only way to God. The Greek word for "I" is *ego*. Their problem was their own self-centeredness, and Paul's answer to that was the humility that belongs to a servant of Christ.

The *third* factor was the overwhelming false loyalty to a particular party leader instead of to Christ. Paul said people don't owe loyalty to a leader. He didn't claim to baptize many himself. Whether one plants or waters, he said, or whatever one does in the name of Christ, all ministry is the same with God. We belong to Christ, not to various divided groups within the fellowship.

We haven't escaped those problems much today, have we? They are still with us. There are those who quickly run up their flags and say they have superior wisdom to that of others. "If you really want to be a Christian," they say, "you've got to bow down to a certain creed, because I have the straight line to God." They claim to know how Christianity is supposed to be understood. This element divides many denominations today. Some are running up their creedal flags that say we must kneel down at the altar of biblical inerrancy and infallibility. Others declare that one must take a "certain" position on abortion, the LGBTQ community, the equality of women in ministry, or some other issue. Their position, they assert, is the only way one can have a right standing with God. They claim to be more orthodox than others. Barbara Brown Taylor quotes the Franciscan father Richard Rohr who says, "We are all of us pointing toward the same moon, and saying we persist in arguing about who has the best finger."[2] How tragic indeed that this force is a part of our denominations today. But it is not the way of Christ. The way of Christ is patience, understanding, and love.

The Problem of Pride

There are people today who are still filled with pride. They are concerned primarily with whether or not they get the recognition in church that they feel they deserve and whether they have their ego needs satisfied. There was a man in a church I pastored once who used to introduce himself to people with this line: "I am the man in this church who keeps things from being unanimous." And he was! He was a constant pain to everybody. He took pride in his difficult spirit because it met some pseudointellectual need for satisfaction, but he was constantly divisive in the church rather than helpful. Notice that Paul tactfully began with the party that had identified with him. What marvelous tact! Paul first confronted the group that said, "I belong to Paul." He set his ego aside and said, "Oh no, you don't. You belong to Christ."

Loyalty Misdirected

There are people today who have loyalty primarily to an individual. If it is not to an individual, sometimes it is to individual programs. Sometimes one's loyalty is to an individual person within a church like a pastor or another staff person. Sometimes an individual is concerned only about the Sunday school, or the music, or the youth program, or recreation, or the weekday program, or the women's program. They have a one-cause mentality. Don't dare talk to them about the whole church or the unity of the church's ministry. Their slogan is "It is my cause above all." They see only one perspective, and that is a part of their divisiveness within the church. I am not saying that these various programs are unimportant. Of course, each one is. But each, as it contributes to the whole ministry, is a part of the body of Christ. The total unity of the church should remain our goal. We should focus on the importance of the parts seen in their proper place as a part of the whole.

How Do We Approach Quarrels in the Church Today?

What do we do about quarrels in the church? Do we say there are no quarrels in today's church? We know better than that, don't we? Can we ignore them and hope they will just go away or pretend that Christians never disagree? We know what happens when we do that. All the hostility is simply buried underground when we refuse to deal with it on the surface. Is there not a better way? Conflict will arise in churches because we are human beings.

Talk about Conflict

We can be willing to talk openly with those with whom we differ. Hopefully, we can go to a brother or sister with whom we differ and talk reasonably with them about our differences, whether it is our understanding of Scripture, church business, or the ministry of the church. We will not deal in rumors and hearsay but instead talk directly with those with whom we disagree. We can have open dialogue with one another and truly listen to each other.

Affirm Differences of Opinion

We can seek to appreciate and understand the opinion of somebody else and recognize that there can be varieties of opinions, understandings, and interpretations within the body of Christ. We can agree that no single theology is necessarily correct for everyone because each of us, especially in the Baptist church and other free churches, is a priest free to interpret the Scriptures for ourselves. No one person, therefore, can say, "I have the only handle on truth, and it is my handle."

Carlyle Marney has an interesting dedication in his book *Faith in Conflict.* The dedication reads like this: "To Victor, who agrees with me in nothing and is my friend in everything." What a marvelous understanding of what it means to be a Christian! Here is one who is able to differ with a brother or a sister and continue in dialogue and a healthy relationship. Though they disagree, they are still friends who know that they do not have to agree on everything. They still recognize that they are brothers and sisters in Christ and still allow another person to have an opinion that differs from their own.

The Church's Goal of Unity

We can strive for the unity of the church. Unity was foremost in the mind of Paul and, more importantly, of Christ. Someone said to me recently that they thought divisiveness was good for the church. That is not true, and it is not biblical. Paul stressed the necessity of the church's unity. "Is the body of Christ divided?" he asked. "Is it fragmented? Is it pulled in all kinds of directions?" To Paul, divisiveness indicated that a person did not understand the essential nature of the Christian faith. Divisiveness, like a tumor, can destroy the body if not removed. Divisiveness is a sign of a "worldly person"—one without Christ. Jesus himself, on the night before he was taken out to be crucified, prayed that his disciples "may be one." *Why?* So the world might "believe that you [God the Father] have sent me." They could not win the world if they were divided like the world. *How?* "That they may all be one; even as You, Father, are in me, and I in You, that they also may be in us, so that the world may believe that You have sent me" (John 17:21). If Christ is in us and we are pulled deeply into the grace of God, then we will not want to be divisive. We will want to be a part of Christ's wholeness and redemption in bringing brothers and sisters into oneness with Christ. We will work not for divisiveness but for unity. We will labor to bring one another together.

Years ago in the fourth century, a young preacher named Arius, who was trained in Antioch, came to Alexandria to preach. He wanted to rise high in the hierarchy of the church of his day. But the church in Alexandria recognized gifts in another young preacher named Alexander, and they made him bishop instead of Arius. Alexander lectured one day to a forum of preachers, and someone asked Arius what he thought about the lecture that day. His comment was,

"Oh, I thought there were going to be some great preachers and teachers here in Alexandria, but he is just a fair to middling preacher. Up in Antioch, where I come from, he would be just a run of the mill preacher. By the way, he also seemed to be promoting a theology which is a little tritheistic. He has a problem properly understanding the Trinity." That day, he set loose a controversy in the church that caused great divisiveness. He spoke out against Alexander to such an extent that the argument grew to the point where a council of the churches met together to resolve it. Arius was banished from the empire for a while. Eventually he was allowed to return. Even after Arius died, though, Athanasius, who became the next bishop, continued to condemn what Arius had said and branded it as heresy. Fifteen hundred years later, preachers who know anything about the doctrines or church history still debate the two sides of the argument.

This tear in the fabric of Christ, about the Trinity, has gone on for centuries and has not been resolved. In many denominations today, one of our great tragedies is that we are fighting over interpretation of Scriptures and other theological viewpoints. We as Christians are waging battles against each other instead of against the forces of evil in the world. I cannot believe that this is what Christ calls us to do as his children. This is not our major assignment, and the result is tragic. Jesus prayed that his children might be one. And yet many continue to strive for division.

The Importance of Humility

We can strive to overcome our pride with humility. When the satisfaction of our pride is our foremost concern, we are far from the spirit of Christ. When our major concern is "Did I get the proper recognition for what I did?" "Did I have the chief seat?" we are far from his spirit. If we say, "I will not serve on any committee unless I am chairperson or unless it in some way gets me significant recognition in the church," then we have not understood what it means to follow Jesus Christ. We still desire first place. Pride is our basic sin.

Charlie Brown is talking to Lucy one day as he is reading the paper. "It says here," he reads, "that young people of today don't believe in any causes," "That's not true at all," Lucy responds. "I believe in a cause. I believe in ME! I'm my OWN cause! If I'm not a cause, what is? I believe in the cause of good ol' ME! THAT'S the cause I believe in! I'M THE BEST CAUSE I KNOW AND I BELIEVE IN THAT CAUSE! I'M THE . . ." Charlie Brown walks off saying, "Good grief."

Many of us see ourselves as the chief cause in everything we do. We want to be sure that we get the proper recognition in what we say or do for Christ in his church, or we won't say or do it. How far removed that is from Christ, who called us to be servants! How far removed that is from the Christ Paul wrote about:

> Have this mind among yourselves, which you have in Christ Jesus who, though he was in the form of God, did not count equality with God a thing to be grasped, but emptied himself, taking the form of a servant, being born in the likeness of men. And being found in human form he humbled himself and became obedient unto death, even death on a cross. (Phil 2:5-8)

How far removed is the spirit of Christ from those who want recognition and first place. Just as he took up the basin and towel to wash his disciples' feet, so he has called us to take them up as symbolic of our servant ministry.

Several decades ago, in the famous Riverside Church in New York City, which Nelson Rockefeller had given the money to build and where Harry Emerson Fosdick was pastor, it was said that in committee meetings heated debates often occurred between Rockefeller and others. Rockefeller would sometimes be forceful in his arguments against why the church should not do certain things or why they should or should not move in a certain direction. When the committee or the church decided to go in a direction diametrically opposed to what he wanted to do, he later would be elected chairman to see that the cause the church chose was carried out. And at that point he would do it with the best grace and dignity of his ability. That is the spirit of Christ at work in his church.

Rockefeller had given millions to build this church, and one day he came in late to a worship service and stood in the lobby by a stranger. The usher said to Mr. Rockefeller, "I'll be glad to take you to your usual seat down front in just a moment." He said, "Oh, no, I don't want to disturb the service. I will go to the balcony." The stranger said, "I'll take the seat. Lead me on down there." What a difference in their spirits! Humility is a sign of the servant of Christ. Pride is overcome by humility. When we understand that we are called to minister and not to be ministered to, how radically different our awareness of the Christian way becomes.

The Way of Love

We can use what Paul calls the "more excellent way" to resolve the problem of quarrels in the church: the way of love. If you really love someone, you do not want to remain upset, disturbed, or isolated from them. If you really love them, you want to be reconciled. You want to make up; you don't want to keep being at odds with them. You want to restore your relationship with them as soon as you can. When the way of love is the Christian way in our hearts and lives, then we seek to do all we can to relate properly to other people. We will not say "I love them" and then do all kinds of divisive things to hurt them. If we love others, we will seek to show it in what we say and do.

A young girl wrapped her arms around her father's neck and hugged him tightly. At the same time, however, she looked over her father's shoulder at her brother and made faces at him and stuck her tongue out at him. Her mother, seeing what she was doing, came over and said, "Take down your arms from your father's neck. Your father loves Tom as much as he loves you; you cannot love your father and make ugly faces at Tom." If you and I are going to put our arms around Christ and let him embrace us, then we cannot stick out our tongues at our brothers and sisters and make faces at them and think we have the spirit of Christ. Paul says, let me tell you about "a more excellent way." His more excellent way is the way of "love." When we love Jesus, we will act lovingly toward others as well.

When Jesus's love dominates our lives, then our first commitment will be to Christ and not to some individual preacher or program. When we truly love Christ, our commitment will show in our treatment and attitude toward others. When his love is dominant in our lives, then hatred, fussing, fighting, arguing, and accusing will not characterize our relationships with others. Love does not desire divisiveness. When we have experienced Christ's love, we will act toward others as Christ has acted toward us in love and grace. We will not hate, hurt, wound, despise, or ridicule another, because that is unlike Christ. Instead, we will love, care, assist, lift up, guide, ease pain, support the weary, comfort the grieving, and forgive the sinner. We will not put down another person; we will reach out to lift them up. We will work to overcome problems, because the power of Christ has permeated our spirits and we are continuously open to his direction.

I like one small girl's definition of the symbolism of the open doors of the church. She said, "When the front doors of the church are opened, it's like we are invited to walk into the very heart of God." When we walk into our church, we should experience the presence of Christ's love, and then we should reach out to others with the power of that love and embrace them with it. Christ has loved us and reconciled us to himself, and he bids us as his children to love as we have been loved.

Christ prayed for the unity of his church, so we pray with him that the church may be one. Paul labored to overcome the divisiveness in the Corinthian church, so we should work to overcome divisiveness in the church today. Just as Christ loved us and we have experienced that love, now we are enabled to reach out and draw others unto ourselves so that we, too, might love as we have been loved. In having been loved, we understand love more effectively. We know that we were loved by God even when we were unlovable, and now we reach out to love those who at times may also be unlovable. But we do it for the love of Christ and the unity of his church.

Chapter 4

The Centrality of the Cross

1 Corinthians 1:18-25

A group of college students gathered together to have a picture taken for their participation in a church retreat. A huge wooden cross served as a backdrop. The photographer asked the students to gather around the cross. Most photographers don't want the people they are photographing simply to stand and look at the camera, so he suggested to the group, "Be adjusting the cross."

These words have stuck with me through the years. Unfortunately, we have done a lot of adjusting of the cross. That suggestion is symbolic of what has happened to our understanding of the cross. We have become casual and indifferent to its message. We don't want much emphasis placed on the cross anymore. People want the church to focus primarily on celebration, peace of mind, comfort, and how to find freedom from worries or problems. Today we have chocolate crosses, candy crosses, and flower crosses. We try to disguise or avoid what the ancient cross meant and continues to mean today.

The Cross Was at the Center of the Preaching of the Early Church

There is no question that the cross was at the center of the preaching about Jesus Christ in the early church. A cross-shaped cavity was found in the wall of an upper room in Pompeii, which was destroyed by Vesuvius in AD 79. About twenty inscriptions of the cross were found in the catacombs at Rome, and scholars date them to the second and third centuries. In most of our churches, the cross is still the central symbol of the Christian faith. The cross is the symbol that is placed on the altar, in stained glass windows, and on the steeple of the church.

In some church traditions a cross is woven into the stoles or other vestments worn by ministers. In some worship settings, the choir processes in and one of the ministers or someone else may carry a processional cross. Some church buildings are constructed in the shape of a cross. Crosses are sometimes imprinted on Bibles, hymn-books, and other religious books. We sing about the cross in our hymns. The cross is depicted in poetry, art, sculpture, and in many other ways.

The Cross Is the Church's Central Symbol

Without question, the cross is the church's central symbol. Yet many people are uncomfortable with the real meaning of the cross symbol. It has once again become an offense to many.

Jürgen Moltmann, a renowned German theologian, wrote the following lines in his scholarly book *The Crucified God*:

> The cross is not and cannot be loved. Yet only the crucified Christ can bring the freedom which changes the world because it is no longer afraid of death. In his time the crucified Christ was regarded as a scandal and foolishness. Today, too, it is considered old-fashioned to put him in the centre of Christian faith and theology. Yet only when men are reminded of him, however untimely this may be, can they be set free from the power of facts of the present time, and from the laws and compulsions of history, and be offered a future which will never grow dark again. Today the church and theology must turn to the crucified Christ in order to show the world the freedom he offers. This is essential if they wish to become what they assert they are: The church of Christ, and Christian theology.[1]

This renowned theologian is reminding the church once again that the cross must be at the center of our faith. Although I have preached many times about the cross, I always stand before it with trembling voice. I struggle to put into words the mystery and awe that encompass the event of the crucifixion. John Milton, who wrote "On the Morning of Christ's Nativity" in celebration of the birth of Jesus, tried to write a similar poem about the cross but finally gave up. There is a mystery about the cross that we can never completely describe. Anyone who says they fully understand what happened at the cross and can explain it sufficiently to somebody else really does not appreciate its mystery.

The Paradox of the Cross

The cross represents a paradox. A paradox is a statement that is seemingly absurd or contradictory. The cross seems inconsistent with common experience. It is paradoxical because it depicts a person at their worst and best. It denotes foolishness and wisdom, a victim and victor, a historical and eternal dimension. A mysterious paradox surrounds the cross and the gospel message that is proclaimed about it. As we attempt to understand the New Testament message on the cross, let us begin by examining Paul's paradoxical statement that the cross is both foolishness and wisdom (1 Cor 1:18-24). Paul noted that to the Jewish mind the cross was a scandal. No Jew expected the Messiah to end up on a cross. The Jewish law stated, "Cursed is he that hangs on a tree" (Deut 21:23). It was a curse to be crucified. The crucifixion was clear evidence to the Jews that Jesus was not the Messiah. They were looking for a political messiah, someone who would come in with military might and strength of arms to overthrow the Roman rulers.

The Scandal of the Cross

The talk about Christ crucified as the Messiah was a stumbling block for the Jewish people. In Greek, the words for "stumbling block" literally mean a trap or snare. The thought of a crucified messiah was a trap that was simply unacceptable. Paul himself persecuted the early Christians because he could not accept this teaching.

In Fyodor Dostoevsky's novel *The Idiot*, a man stands before a copy of Holbein's painting *Christ in the Tomb* and says he likes looking at it. Another character cries, "At that painting? A man could even lose his faith from that painting!" "Lose it he does," the first character replies.[2]

The cross was seen as such a scandal that the Jewish people rejected any notion of a crucified Messiah. To the Greeks, on the other hand, the concept of a crucified God was considered plain foolishness. The Greeks took pride in their rational knowledge and logical understanding of life. The word "foolishness" is derived from a Greek word that is the root for our word "moron." The Greeks ridiculed anyone who believed that a crucified carpenter could bring salvation.

The disdain the Greeks held for the cross was depicted in a painting discovered on an ancient wall. When the plaster was removed, a figure was seen hanging on a cross. The figure had the body of a man and the head of an ass. Underneath were the words "Alex the Jew worships his god." The Greeks directed this kind of disdain and ridicule at the early Christians because they believed that the concept of a crucified Christ was totally absurd.

The Cross as the Power of God

Paul is bold to declare that what seems like a scandal and foolishness to others is actually the power and wisdom of God. The cross is the power of God because it is an expression of God's sacrificial love. Although it sounded foolish, Paul affirmed, "Unto us which are saved it is the power of God." He preached that God's strength was made perfect in Paul's weakness. The cross event revealed God's power in a unique way. God's power is consistent with God's character. God does not exercise raw power or try to coerce or force people's love; God draws people in with love.

In the upper room Jesus gave his disciples a strange picture of power. He, knowing that all power in heaven and on earth was his, took a towel and a basin and washed his disciples' feet like a slave (John 13:3-11). His power was dedicated to service. Jesus said on another occasion, "Whoever would be chief among you, let him be the slave or servant of all" (Matt 20:27). In Jesus, God's power was focused in the form of a servant. This is disciplined power—the power of sacrificial love.

The New Testament is filled with many images that the various writers employ to depict the power of God revealed in the cross of Christ. Paul used the image of justification, which he took from the law courts. He drew pictures of redemption and emancipation from the slave market, reconciliation from the image of friendship, adoption from family life, propitiation or ransom from the sacrificial system of Judaism, sanctification from their worship practices, and the view of setting a person's account right from the accounting system. Many theologians have built their theological system around one of these pictures.

A Variety of Images Interpret the Cross

But the New Testament does not give just one interpretation of Christ's death on the cross. There are many. A casual glimpse into the New Testament discloses images of Christ's death as sacrifice, substitution, metaphors drawn from the law courts, expiation, forensic, satisfaction, example, revelation, deliverer, representative, suffering servant, lamb, and many others.

No single one of these images contains all of the truth about what God has done in Christ's death. All of these images underscore the great mystery involved in the God who has loved and redeemed us on the cross. The cross can never be reduced to simple images like legal or judicial interactions, transferring of guilt, paying off a debt, contracts with the devil, appeasing an angry God, etc. These images are just illustrations of the power and mystery of what God has done in Christ on the cross. No one of these pictures can contain the whole of the mystery.

The Cross as the Wisdom of God

The cross is not only the "power of God," according to Paul; it is the "wisdom of God" as well. Unlike many itinerant Greek teachers of wisdom who emphasized rhetoric and eloquence, Paul declared that he proclaimed "an unadorned gospel." The Greeks wanted something that would satisfy the mind, but the images of God on a cross blew their minds. The wisdom of God that Paul is describing could never be reduced to a system of beliefs about God or to a set of proposi-tions. This wisdom was personally revealed through Christ's death within history.

The word "mystery" here is not a reference to something that remains unknown or a puzzle but refers to what was previously unknown. The reference is to the redemptive work of God in Christ. Something that was previously unknown about God's nature has been revealed through the death of Christ. "To those who have been called, both Jew and Greek, Christ is the power of God and the wisdom of God, for the foolishness of God is wiser than men, and the weakness of God is stronger than men" (1 Cor 1:24-25). In a unique way, Christ has revealed the power and wisdom of God's love.

The Cross and Sin

The cross also reveals to us something about the ugliness of sin. Sin is so costly that God's Son went to the cross to lay down his life for us. We are all too familiar with our own sense of sin. We are never free from it.

You may have seen the *Peanuts* cartoon where Lucy walks over to Snoopy one day and says, "Hold my balloon. I'm going to lunch." She sticks the string in his mouth and walks away. He sits there holding the string with his teeth, and the balloon floats above his head. A few minutes later he falls asleep. When he awakens suddenly, he yawns and lets go of the string. The balloon drifts off as the wind carries it up into the sky. In the last scene Snoopy is walking down some railroad tracks with a little parcel on his shoulder. "Make one mistake," he observes, "and you have to regret it all your life."

Many of us go through life with a sense of regret over mistakes we have made, and we wonder what we can do to overcome these feelings or find forgiveness. The good news of the gospel is that you and I never have to try to overcome our sins with our own strength. Through God's grace, revealed in the mystery of the cross, we find forgiveness and the opportunity to begin anew.

A small boy went to church for the first time one Sunday. He saw a cross on the altar and nudged his mother and asked, "Mother, what is that plus mark doing on that table?" That may not be a bad image to use to describe the cross. The cross is God's "plus" mark that reveals God's affirmation, love, grace, and forgiveness. Yes, the cross is a paradox. It is foolishness to those who think they can solve all of life's problems with their own efforts and strength. But it is also the mysterious wisdom of God's love and atonement.

Jesus as Victim and Victor

The cross is a paradox because it reveals that in his death, Jesus was both victim and victor. The New Testament states that Jesus's life was both taken and given. The cross represents suffering and triumph, defeat and victory, horror and glory, wickedness and sacrifice. The cross shows that in one way Jesus was a victim. He was betrayed by Judas. He was rejected by the religious leaders, scourged, and put to death by Roman officials. The cross depicts murder, betrayal, and rejection. "The stone which the builders rejected," Jesus said, "has become the head of the corner" (Mark 12:10). The New Testament clearly states that Jesus was betrayed and murdered. (See Acts 2:23; 2:36; 7:52; 13:28; 1 Thess 2:15-16.) Marcus Borg denotes the varied dimensions of the cross when he describes "the cross as a trustworthy disclosure of the evil of domination systems, as the exposure of the defeat of the powers, as the revelation of the 'way' or 'path' of transformation, as the revelation of the depth of God's love for us and as the proclamation of radical grace."[3]

From one perspective the death of Jesus means a life that was taken, but the New Testament never leaves it there. The biblical writers are bold to declare that he was not just a victim but also a victor. They believed that he was in charge of what was happening. Listen to the words of Jesus himself: "For this reason the Father loves me, because I lay down my life that I may take it again. No one takes it from me, but I lay it down of my own accord. I have power to lay it down and I have power to take it again; this charge I received from my Father" (John 10:17-18). Then in Mark's Gospel Jesus says, "The Son of man also came not to be served but to serve, and to give his life as a ransom for many" (Mark 10:45).

On another occasion Jesus said, "I am the good shepherd and I lay down my life for the sheep" (John 10:15). When he was approaching Jerusalem, Jesus looked down on the town and wept, saying, "O Jerusalem, Jerusalem, killing the prophets and stoning those who have been sent to you! How often would I have gathered your children together as a hen gathers her brood under her wings, and you would not!" (Matt 23:37). Jesus wept over Jerusalem, but there is no indication that Jerusalem wept for him.

After Peter's confession at Caesarea Philippi (Mark 8:29), Jesus warned his disciples that he had to suffer and die. Following the transfiguration, at the Last Supper, and on other numerous occasions, Jesus told his disciples that he would go to Jerusalem and die. But they never seemed to hear or understand his prediction. It was only after the resurrection that his disciples began to sense what he had taught them. When Jesus the risen Lord was walking with two of his disciples on the road to Emmaus, he said, "Oh fools, and slow of heart to believe all that the prophets have spoken. Was it not necessary that Christ should suffer these things?" (Luke 24:25-26). Then he opened the Scriptures to them and interpreted from the prophets and other writings the prophecies of how the Messiah must suffer many things. Have you ever wondered what particular passages Jesus must have shared with those disciples that day? Did he quote from the Psalms, Jeremiah, and Isaiah? Paul, writing later to the Corinthians, declared, "For I delivered to you as of first importance what I also received, that Christ died for our sins in accordance with the Scriptures" (1 Cor 15:3).

Jesus was not merely a victim; he was also a victor. The Old Testament Scriptures do indeed predict the suffering One who would be God's Messiah. Israel did not seem to look for such a Messiah, but what other image could one draw from Isaiah? Isaiah's image is clearly about a Suffering Messiah. Listen to the verbs in Isaiah's passage about the Suffering Servant in the fifty-third chapter. He will be marred, recoiled, shut-mouthed, avoided, afflicted, bearing our sufferings, enduring our torments, smitten by God, struck down by disease and misery, wounded, bruised, chastised, crushed, oppressed, dumb, stricken to death, numbered with transgressors, bearing the sins of many, offered for sin, pouring out his soul, and making his grave with the wicked. The verbs disclose something about the suffering, sacrificial nature of the One who would give his life. These verbs vibrate with the heartbeat of a Suffering One and are not the vision of a militant king.

Sacrifice as a Vital Part of the Church's Life

Suffering has always been at the heart of the life of the church, and that is still true today. Sometimes we want to put sacrifice on the back burner, but we really cannot do this and still be the church. I am convinced that nothing worthwhile ever comes about in life without some kind of sacrifice. To serve or reach worthy goals, there has to be some sacrifice of time, energy, effort, or money, and sometimes even of one's life.

Several years ago, when I was visiting a church member who had been ill, his wife told me about a couple in our church who had visited them recently. She spoke kindly of this visit and of how much it had meant to them. She observed how many others this couple also visited. I thought about the numerous lives this couple touched because they were willing to sacrifice time to visit the sick or home-bound. But they were willing to pay that price. The Christian gospel continues to focus on the necessity of sacrifice.

The Cross as Historical and Eternal

The Gospel writers also denote that there was both a historical and an eternal dimension to the cross. In one way, the cross is a historical event because Christ was crucified at a certain date, place, and time. The date was approximately AD 30. Jesus was crucified on the garbage dump outside Jerusalem at Golgotha. Beyond the city gate, Jesus was crucified between two thieves. George McLeod of Iona reminds us of the historical nature of the cross in these words:

> I simply argue that the cross be raised again at the center of the market place, as well as on the steeple of the church. I am recovering the claim that Jesus was not crucified on a cathedral between two candles, but on a cross between two thieves; on the town's garbage heap, at the crossroads so cosmopolitan that they had to write his title in Hebrew and in Latin and in Greek, at the kind

of place where cynics talk smut and thieves cursed and soldiers gambled . . . . That is where he died and that is what he died about.[4]

Christ died in a particular place at a particular time. But the Scriptures are also clear that Christ's death was not merely a historical event; there was an eternal dimension to the death of Christ. God did not suddenly become loving at the cross in the death of Jesus. God has always been a loving God. The book of Revelation states that Jesus was "the Lamb that was slain from the foundation of the world" (Rev 13:8). Here is the image of the cross that was always at the heart of God before it was planted on a hillside. The cross discloses the heart of God. The cross provides a clear picture of a God who is eternally loving and caring. Jesus did not have to persuade God to love people and be reconciled to them, but he revealed that his death was to persuade us to be reconciled to God who already loved us. God's work of redemption continues into every age. This is the truth Emil Brunner noted when he wrote,

> The Atonement is not history. The Atonement, the expiation of human guilt, the covering of sin through His sacrifice is not anything which can be conceived from the point of view of history. This event does not belong to the historical plane. It is super-history; it lies in the dimension which no historian knows in so far as he is a mere historian.[5]

As we reflect on the cross, it tells us about the death of Jesus in a particular place at a particular time, but the cross also reveals to us a God who is continuously loving, redeeming, and suffering and who makes grace available to us today.

Paul said the Jews seek a sign—a miracle—and the Greeks want wisdom, but we preach Christ crucified. We—everyone who proclaims the message of salvation—testify and bear witness to Christ. We witness to a person, not a philosophy or a system of theological thought. We preach Christ crucified. He is not just an example or a teacher or a martyr. We preach Christ crucified—God's Suffering Servant who laid down his life for us.

Following the death of French author Victor Hugo, there was a riot, and the French people secularized the Pantheon. They pulled down the gilded cross because they wanted to remove all evidence of Christianity from the building. A Christian orator stood up and tried to stop them. "You think you can take away the cross from the Pantheon," he cried. "We have taken it away," they shouted. "We've torn it down." "You'll never take away the cross from the Pantheon," the Christian orator shouted. "It is taken away, and down with the church," they yelled. After the shouting died down, he stated quietly, "You cannot take away the cross from the Pantheon, for the Pantheon is built in the form of a cross, and when you have taken away the cross, there will be no Pantheon anymore."[6]

To remove the cross from Christianity is to destroy the Christian message. The cross is at the center of our message about Christ. If we remove the cross from Christianity, we do not have the genuine New Testament message. With the hymn writer Isaac Watts, let us proclaim,

When I survey the wondrous cross
On which the prince of glory died,
My richest gain I count but loss,
And pour contempt on all my pride.
Forbid it, Lord, that I should boast,
Save in the death of Christ, my God.[7]

Chapter 5

Being Moral in an Immoral World

1 Corinthians 6:9–20

"Who would know?" the young woman asked herself. "My husband is off in the service, and I am lonely. My boss has been good to me. He has invited me to go with him to his cottage in the mountains for the weekend. No one else would ever know. Why not?" She struggled with the kind of issue that many often face. She was confronted with the question of moral decisions. Some people view life mostly in shades of gray. For others, it seems to be painted in black colors. We can pick up the morning paper and read about bank robberies, or about someone running off with the company funds, or about some industries being sued due to chemicals that they have dumped into our waters, or about drug companies being sued due to false claims that they have made for their products. We read that a man has raped and killed dozens of women and has no sense of remorse, or that a teenager on drugs killed some of his best friends, or that a student shot teachers and other students. We read that people are willing to lie and cheat their way in business and in preparing their income tax forms, striving to get by any way they can.

We Make Moral Decisions Every Day

Some people have turned white lies into black lies and every shade in between because for them morality has nothing to do with reality. We face moral decisions on every corner. What are we to do? A football team may have already been given their orders by the coach on what they should do to get the place kicker into the game with just a few seconds left and no timeouts remaining. At the appropriate time, the coach's plan is put into action and the right guard rolls over, pretending that he has something wrong with his leg. When the officials stop the game and come over to give assistance to him, it gives the coach time to get the place kicker onto the field. Later, as the ball goes through the uprights, someone notices that the young man whose leg seemed to be in such pain a few moments before is now leading the cheers and jumping up and down.

A mother is in the grocery store doing her weekly shopping, and her young child takes a package of cookies off the shelf and eats a portion of them while the mother is distracted by the shelves of goods. When the mother turns around and notices that her daughter has consumed half the package, she folds it up and puts it back on the shelf and then goes through the line and pays for her groceries. Several people who witnessed what the child did call it to the attention of the clerk. But the mother denies it. Contrast that with the father who brings his child back to the store to teach him a lesson because he took a candy bar and didn't pay for it.

A television executive announces that what we need on TV is more violence and more nudity. Many of our contemporary films exploit sex and violence, linking them together in the minds of viewers and planting seeds in the heads of young people that violence and sex go together. Is it any wonder that society is distorted by such media?

A high school student realizes that she does not know the answers to the geometry test, and sitting right in front of her is the smartest guy in the class, his paper uncovered. All she has to do is look and she can see the answers.

Moral struggles do not always happen in a faraway world. One of the most disarming disclosures that came to me was a sign I saw several years ago in the seminary bookstore: "Please stop stealing the Bibles." A student was also caught leaving the campus bookstore after stealing a book on Christian ethics. The seminary later installed a monitoring system as students left the library because of the many stolen books. What does this indicate about our ethical breakdown?

What has happened to the morals in our world when even ministerial students do not have morals?

Shades of Gray

For many, moral values seem to be painted not in clear colors but in shades of gray. There is nothing that appears in black or white anymore. It all appears multicolored, and you and I are told to take our choice and pick whatever color we may want. We are told to live on the raw edge. After all, we only go around once. We are only young once. Forget caution, we are told; don't be old-fashioned. This is your day, so express yourself. Take your last fling; enjoy life. Eat, drink, and be merry. We are living in a day and age in which moral standards are not lifted high for all people. Our moral values have slipped, and too often we are mirrors of the society around us.

A young bride was fixing her first ham. She cut off both ends of the ham before she placed it in the oven. Her husband asked, "Why do you cut off both ends of the ham?" "Well, my mother has always done that," she replied, "and I'm just doing what she did." The next time the couple was over at her mother's house, the son-in-law asked her, "Why do you cut off both ends of the ham before you put it in the oven?" "Well, it's the only way I can get the ham to fit in the size pan I have," she responded.

Too many people in the world today are trying to cut off both ends of issues to make them fit into pans of conformity that are too small. Others have taken the values of our society and cut the ends off and reduced their standards to the level of doing what they want. These people live by the rule, "If it makes you feel good, do it." "If it feels okay to me," they say, "is it really hurting anybody else?"

Test Your Values

Paul faced this kind of problem in the Corinthian church (see 1 Cor 6:9-20). He was writing to a people who claimed to be Christians but also had corrupt moral standards. He challenged them to be moral in an immoral society. He asked them first to test their slogan, "Everything is lawful." "Test that slogan," he said, "to see whether it is true."

"I am free to do anything," they said. "Yes," he affirmed, "that is true to an extent. We are free to do anything, but everything you may do may not be helpful for you. It may not be helpful to others, and using your freedom with absolute license may in turn cause harm to you and to others in society."

Then Paul began some of his pointed statements: "Do you not know . . . ?" He asked them, "Do you not know that when you link your life with a prostitute you distort your own body because you engage in corrupt behavior?" Some of the Corinthians thought it did not make any difference what a person did with his body because one day the body would die, and only the spirit would live on. They thought that anything they wanted to do was okay. The body was not a real concern—only one's motive or intent. Paul declared that this was not true. When your body is linked with prostitution, he said, it too becomes corrupted. He asked, "Do you not know that you are the temple of God? Do you not know that you are supposed to glorify God in your body? Yes, you have freedom, but you don't have freedom to do anything you want. You must see how you use your freedom in relationship to God and to other people." When we treat others as less than people, we have not only distorted them but also ourselves. When we engage in any kind of immoral behavior, we distort our bodies.

Some try to focus on selected Scripture verses like 1 Corinthians 6:9, 1 Timothy 1:10, and Romans 1:28-32 to "prove" that homosexuality in particular is unforgivable, and they ignore the other issues that Paul enumerates as sinful. The major problem with this isolated reading is that many scholars note that the Greek word interpreted to mean "homosexual" in these passages is a word that Paul seems to have "coined" for these letters to address the sexual immorality and bad behavior occurring in the early church. Some have proposed that a better rendering of this rare word might be sexual exploiters, rapists, sexual predators, or pimps. Paul was concerned with all the sexual "looseness" that was transpiring in the church, along with drunkenness, idolatry, thievery, greed, robbery, etc. Do we likewise condemn such people to hell without the possibility of forgiveness? In the very next verse, Paul indicates that these sins used to indicate the nature of the people to whom he is writing, but God has justified them in Christ Jesus (6:11).

The attempt to label homosexuality a sin denies the reality that being gay is not a choice one makes but is the way one is born. Scientists indicate that it is genetic. To try to get a gay person to undergo what is called "conversion therapy" is to declare that something is not right with that person and that they need to change. Studies have shown that the so-called "conversion therapy," often harsh and abusive, does not work because a person cannot change how they were born. LGBTQ people are God's children, and the church needs to recognize this and acknowledge that everyone can experience God's love, grace, and forgiveness.

Paul is warning the church at Corinth not to continue in its pattern of sexual looseness. To continue in this way, he asserts, will not lead to a path of forgiveness but to continuous sinning. I read about a judge in Kentucky who used a certain test for sanity. This test was simple: A person was brought into a room, and a bucket of water was placed in front of him with a spigot above it turned on to allow the water to run into the bucket. The man was asked to empty the bucket of water with a dipper. If the man tried to empty the bucket of water without first turning off the spigot, the judge knew that the man was not sane.

Part of our problem in society is that we, like an insane man facing the water bucket test, are trying to correct our moral problems without getting back to the source and turning them off. Part of the origin of our problems is the belief in absolute freedom. Absolute freedom is a myth because no one can do anything they may want to do without regard for other people. My actions and your actions involve others, and we are never totally isolated in what we say or do in any particular moment.

Rules Have Their Place

Rules are important. But people are more important than rules. Jesus indicated that people were more important than regulations about the Sabbath Day, more important than the rigid legalism of the Jewish system that focused on minor details of the law. But Jesus did give us some principles about life in the Sermon on the Mount and in his other teachings. His teachings offer guidance on how we are to think about ourselves and how to relate to others in society. To say that there are no rules by which Christians live and that each person is free to make up their own rules is to misrepresent the Christian faith. The Ten Commandments are still valid as basic guidelines for living. To follow Christ effectively, we seek to incorporate the principles of his life and teachings into our own lives.

A father of twelve children who lived in a house with only one bathroom once said: "Rules are not an option here. They are a necessity!" And so are moral principles.

Morality Needs to Touch All of Society

When we try to live in the world, rules are not just optional; they are essential. This is true not only in individual relationships but especially when we move to the wider dimension of society at large. What I do privately not only affects me but also touches other people. In society, I may live a private moral life, but my morality must also move into the business world where I work and into the industrial and financial world in which I am involved.

Over eighty years ago Reinhold Niebuhr, one of the great moral theologians of the last century, wrote a book titled *Moral Man and Immoral Society*. In this book, he addressed the issue of morality in one's private life and the difference in morality in our business, industrial, national, and other collective areas. People can often do very immoral things in the collective areas of life and never recognize that their actions are wrong. Niebuhr's challenge echoes the biblical demand that morality is an absolute necessity in our business practice and in all our public lives as well as in our private interactions with others. Morality is not limited to one's private life, as important as that is; moral values should permeate our relationships in business, industry, government, and other institutions. The prophet Amos exemplified this when he cried for justice in the land of Israel: "Seek good and not evil . . . Hate evil and love good; enthrone justice in the courts" (Amos 5:14-15, NEB).

Morality Is Grounded in God

Paul also says that our morality is linked with God. We are "God's temple," he said. "Glorify God with your body." Our morality is directly related to God. Morality is not merely what we think is correct in the moment. Too many people depend on their conscience alone. They assume that if they think something is the decent thing to do, that makes it okay. They declare that they will let conscience be the guide. I am sometimes troubled by people who want to follow their conscience, because their conscience does not seem morally strong enough to give them the kind of guidance they need for a valid decision.

In John Galsworthy's novel *Maid in Waiting*, there is a scene in which Dinny is talking with her mother about God and daily living.

"Providence is a wash-out, Mother," Dinny says. "It's too remote. I suppose there is an eternal Plan—but we're like gnats for all the care it has for us as individuals."

"Don't encourage such feelings, Dinny; they affect one's character," her mother responds.

"I don't see the connection between beliefs and character," Dinny replies. "I'm not going to behave any worse because I cease to believe in Providence or an after life . . . . No; I'm going to behave *better*, if I'm decent it's because decency's the decent thing; and not because I'm going to get anything by it."

"But why is decency the decent thing, Dinny," her mother asks, "if there's no God?"[1]

That is the question, isn't it? When we push decency back far enough and remove it from any relationship to spirituality and God, we begin to see shades of gray creeping in as morality is determined by every passing fad and contemporary notion. Many views of decency are based merely on social customs of right and wrong without relating them to God. The present generation that seeks to live a decent life may have been influenced by parents who believed in God and the moral goodness revealed in Christ. Some of them may have drifted away from God and the church, so what "rootage" for their morality will they pass on to their children? When decency has no spiritual rootage, it is based primarily on what an individual thinks is right or wrong. I am frightened of those who want to let their conscience be their primary guide. Some people have too easily and quickly let their conscience become twisted and distorted by all kinds of negative influences.

During World War II, while being trained at Kelly Field, young pilots were told by their instructors that they had to learn to trust their instruments implicitly or they would be killed. One day a pilot was flying in a storm, and he kept feeling like his plane's right wing was too low. He continued to pull it up more and more until he felt his straps pressing tightly against his body. He couldn't understand why they were so tight. He wanted to loosen them when he got a moment. Then suddenly he thought, "I had better look at my instruments." When he did, he saw that he was flying upside down in the wrong direction. The words came home to him from his instructor: "Fly by your instrument board. Trust it and not your feelings."

Too many people rely on their own feelings about what is right, and they have not grounded themselves in a vital relationship to Jesus Christ, who gives direction on how to live. We go off on our own without clear direction or certain standards. It should not be just our opinion; we should look to Christ as the model and guide for ethical behavior.

A Christian's Walk Will Be Different

When my life is related to God, I am going to live differently because of that connection. As Paul said, "You are not your own. You are bought with a price." Part of his reference was to the fact that the people in this early Corinthian church lived in a city where temples were built to love goddesses. The prostitutes of this love goddess would often walk the streets and solicit trade, and some of the Christians would pay the prostitute and engage in sex with her. Paul condemned this act and warned them that they had identified themselves with prostitutes and become one with them. That union was wrong, Paul believed, because such unity was reserved for the sexual relationship within marriage. Otherwise, in the eyes of God it is sin. There is no such thing as casual sex.

There is no such thing as moral sex with a prostitute either. This relationship distorts and twists one's life. We cannot say, "I can be sexually involved with somebody other than my mate and it doesn't make any difference," because it does. There is no such thing as a simple physical relationship. Paul knew that our physical relationship affects our spiritual life. Casual sex corrupts and destroys one's spiritual life.

You Are Bought with a Price

Paul said, "You are bought with a price." Often when we hear that phrase, we think Paul is writing about the ransom Christ gave for us. But John Ruef, a New Testament scholar, believes that the real reference here is still to prostitution. Just as one would pay a prostitute and use her as he wanted, so one had been bought by God and now belonged to God. Through this crass analogy, Paul calls Christians to glorify God in our bodies. Ruef acknowledges that this might not be "a very delicate way of putting it but the Corinthians (to whom Paul was writing) were probably not very delicate people."[2] Paul's words strike with force and clarity: "Live your life without being related in this corrupt way to prostitutes so that you can walk in purity with Christ." Paul calls Christians to remember that they do not *have* a body but they *are* a body. Spirit and body are intertwined.

I have often wondered whether we would do certain things if we first gave them the publicity test. How would you like for certain acts or deeds that you have done to be reported in the local newspaper, on local television, on Facebook, or in the newsletter of your church or community? None of us may want some of our dark deeds done in the shadows to be seen by the public eye. But one of the tests for our morality might be this: "Can it stand the test of daylight and exposure in the public arena? Can it stand the public test of those around me—my friends and others? Do I want these private acts to be known in public circles?"

Some politicians have gotten into great difficulty because of indiscreet acts they engaged in earlier in life. So you and I should seek to live in such a way that our lives are not destroyed later by the acts we may do in the darkness or in times of weakness. Let the test of publicity remind us that our moral lives are evidence that we have been bought with a price and that we are seeking to glorify God in our bodies.

Live on a Higher Plane

Paul says that if we have committed our lives to Christ, and if we are seeking to let our bodies be God's holy temple, then we are called to live on a higher plane in the world. We shall not live like those who are without Christ. We shall live as moral people in an immoral society. We do not live like the crowd, but Christ is our model and guide, and we live like him. We follow the narrow way and march to the beat of a different drummer. We follow the One who upholds a higher standard. We shall seek to be his light and salt in the world so that people can see by our walk with Christ that we are radically different.

I read several years ago about how a small animal, the ermine, is captured in the wintertime. In summer, this small creature's fur is brown all over except for a white spot on its tail, but in winter its fur becomes snow white. When hunters want to capture this animal, they simply force it toward the mud pits. When the animal with its beautiful white fur gets close to the mud pit, it yields up its life rather than soil its fur.

I wonder if we have understood the high moral demands of Christ. "Glorify God in your body." "You are God's temple." Will we stop before the forces of evil and corruption because we do not want to be spotted and tainted by them? We are challenged to stand in the courageous tradition with Moses before Pharaoh, with Jesus before Pilate, with Paul before King Agrippa, with Luther before the Roman bishops, with John Bunyan before the English courts, with Martin Niemoller before Hitler, and with Martin Luther King Jr. before the white establishment. These people stood up for their convictions at great personal cost. They were not corrupted as they let right prevail.

A Christian should not be willing to say, "I will go along with what everybody else does." As a Christian, there are values in your life for which you will stand, and you will not be persuaded to move away from them. We need people with this kind of integrity in business, in government, and in every walk of life. We need people in public places whose integrity is without question, whose word is their bond, and who can be trusted and relied on to do what they promise.

A moving play for me is the one by Thomas Bolt titled *A Man for All Seasons*. In this play, Sir Thomas More is appointed Archbishop of Canterbury. Henry VIII has married Catherine, a princess of Spain, and ascended the English throne as king. Later he grows tired of her and wants to divorce her because she cannot bear him male heirs. He requests that the archbishop approve his marriage to Anne Boleyn, after he has rejected Catherine. More refuses to do this because it would require him to state that he believes what he does not really believe, and he would have to declare it with an oath. More is placed in prison. All kinds of pressures are put upon him to commit perjury. He is told that if he does not agree to the king's demands, he will be put to death. His daughter Margaret comes to prison and pleads with her father, begging him to sign the oath and save his life.

> More: You want me to swear to the Act of Succession?
> Margaret: God more regards the thoughts of the heart than the words of the mouth. Or so you've always told me.
> More: Yes.
> Margaret: Then say the words of the oath and in your heart think otherwise.
> More: What is an oath then but words we say to God?
> Margaret: That's very neat.
> More: Do you mean it isn't true?
> Margaret: No, it's true.
> More: Then it's a poor argument to call it "neat," Meg. When a man takes an oath, Meg, he's holding his own self in his own hands. Like water. (*He cups his hands.*) And if he opens his fingers then he needn't hope to find himself again. Some men aren't capable of this, but I'd be loathe to think your father one of them.[3]

We need more people—men and women—who have high standards, strong convictions, and high moral values, who have modeled their lives after Christ and are not carried away by every wind of popular appeal and corruption that comes along. These are the people who have determined to let Christ be the standard for their lives and to follow him. That is not always easy. Many forces constantly pull at us.

I heard about a woman who had lost her sense of touch. She could place her hand on a hot stove and be burned badly because she could not feel it. Her hand could be literally frozen to a block of ice because she could not feel the pain. A pin could be stuck in her hand, and she could not feel it. That is a great tragedy and danger. What an even greater tragedy it would be for those of us who are supposed to be children of God to lose our sense of feeling for what is right and wrong. May Paul, in his words to the Corinthian church, remind us that we have been bought with a price and are consecrated to God, and therefore we are challenged to glorify God through our bodies. My prayer is that we will not lose our sense of value for what is morally right and that we shall daily bear witness to the Christ we serve.

Chapter 6

The Illusion of Freedom
1 Corinthians 9:1–23

One day a man wanted to build a tool shed near his home. He was informed, however, that he could not construct a wooden building because the neighborhood had a restriction that permitted only brick structures. He wasn't pleased with that restriction, but he finally had to give in to it only to be told that he must get a permit for his construction. "I absolutely refuse to do that," he said, but he soon discovered that he could not build his shed unless he got a permit. After he paid for the permit, he was so disgusted that he went out and spat on the sidewalk. When he did that, a police officer was standing nearby and arrested him. The man had to go to the courthouse and pay a fine for that action. This made him so angry that he got in his car and raced down the road and went through a red light. A policeman pulled him over and he had to go back and pay a fine. He got so frustrated with the community that he exclaimed, "I absolutely refuse to live in such a town as this." As he got to the city limits, he was stopped by the city health inspector who said, "Sorry, you can't leave this town. It is quarantined because of smallpox."

The Illusion of Absolute Freedom

We, like this man, all live with an illusion of absolute freedom. But it doesn't exist. Absolute freedom is nonexistent, though most of us constantly long for it. Some have even taken Paul's phrase, "I am all things to all men," to mean that we can really do anything we want to do. In our society today, the prodigal son from Jesus's parable has become a patron saint of many people (Luke 15). "Give me my share so I can go do my thing any place I want to at any time," they cry.

Unfortunately, too many have bought into the idea that is depicted in much of our media: "Free sex and permissiveness make life worthwhile. Do whatever you want. Do your own thing. This is a free country." But is life really that free?

Fyodor Dostoevsky, the Russian writer, once penned, "Without God everything is permissible." But with a spiritual presence to direct us, everything is not okay. The Apostle Paul quotes a common refrain of his day in 1 Corinthians 10:23: "Everything is permissible." And then he adds his own words: "but not all things build up." Paul did not mean that he could do anything he wanted to at any time without any consequences. In 1 Corinthians 9, he explains that he has learned something about adaptability. He has learned how to relate to people where they are. Paul was Jewish, and he knew that if he was to have an opportunity to reach the Jewish people, he had to continue with some of the Jewish traditions so he would not alienate them. He had Timothy circumcised, although he knew it wasn't essential for a Christian. He felt like that part of the law did not need to be fulfilled, but he went ahead and permitted circumcision for Timothy rather than alienate his Jewish friends (see Acts 16). When Paul gave interpretations of the Scriptures before some Jewish listeners, he used a traditional Jewish rabbinical way of allegorizing a passage about Hagar and Sarah (see Galatians 4).

An Understandable Appeal

To appeal to the Gentiles, Paul often used images from their athletic races, Greek attire, the dress and equipment of a soldier, and the Olympic games. He even quoted from a few Gentile poets in some of his letters. He tried to relate the gospel to the Gentiles in languages and themes that would draw them into conversation about life and God. On Mars Hill he gave a philosophical address on the resurrection in hope of reaching the inquiring Greek mind (see Acts 17). To those who were weaker in the faith, he tried to live his life in such a way as not to cause them to stumble. He believed that eating meat offered to idols did not make any difference to him, because he knew that the idols were not true gods. But some people were still struggling with that issue, and Paul did not want the eating of this meat to cause anyone to stumble.

What is Paul saying in 1 Corinthians 9? He is attempting to adapt the gospel to people where they are. We need to continue to do that today. Some people who never get out of the King James Version of the Bible in their view of interpretations do not understand why many people today never read the Scriptures. Most people do not understand the language of the KJV. Nobody talks like that today, with all of the "thees" and "thous." That is one of the reasons it is essential to use images, illustrations, and metaphors to interpret Scripture for people in the world where they live today. Paul did that kind of image translation for his listeners, and Jesus did it before him.

The Goal of Reaching People for Christ

Notice that Paul had a particular reason for this strategy. His purpose was not to do anything anywhere at any time; his purpose was to win people to Christ. He spoke to the Jewish people using their familiar images in order to help them more thoroughly understand what Christ meant to the Jewish people. He wanted the Gentiles to see how Jesus Christ was God's revelation to all people. He wanted those who were strong to bear up those who were weaker. The strong were challenged to bear the burdens of others. He attempted to relate the gospel to many people in ways they could clearly grasp.

The Necessity of Discipline

Paul knew well the significance and value of discipline. He had disciplined his life to follow Christ. This discipline was evident again and again in the sacrifices he made as he committed himself to serving Christ. He disciplined himself to Christ's ways.

There is no authentic life without discipline. We all live with some kind of discipline. We discover early that there is no such thing as absolute freedom. We have the freedom to do certain things, but when we do them, we have to suffer the consequences of those actions. I am limited and so are you. If the temperature rises above a certain degree, then I will die. If the temperature goes below a certain degree, I will also die, and so will you. Our bodies cannot survive at too high or too low a temperature. We do not have the freedom to live at any temperature. Space suits and other equipment can help us survive at some levels and for some period of time. Without that artificial means, we cannot make it. If I climb to the top of the bell tower and jump off, I cannot decide halfway down that I do not want to do that. The law of gravity will be enforced. Fish cannot swim in the air, and neither can most birds swim under the water. There are limits. Fish are adapted to live in the water, and birds can fly in the air. Each creature learns to be where it is supposed to be.

I cannot go anyplace I want to. I am not absolutely free to travel anywhere. First, I don't have enough money to go anywhere I want. Second, I don't have the time. Third, I don't have the languages to go every place. Fourth, I can't get a passport to go some places; our country will not permit it. Fifth, some countries today will not permit me to enter. We are not absolutely free to go anyplace we want to, because others put restrictions on us.

Society puts restrictions on us too. You cannot stand up in a building and yell "fire" if there is no fire. That is against the law, and you'd likely be arrested. In a public building, you are not free to do anything you want. You are not free to walk into a store and fill up your grocery cart and roll it out to your car and load the groceries into your trunk without stopping by the cash register. If you try that, then you have to suffer the consequences that society has imposed. None of us is absolutely and totally free. I am bound by my education. You do not want me to perform brain surgery on you. I am not educated or equipped for that. You do not want me to design a nuclear submarine. I am not prepared for that. Our education puts some limitations on us. Heredity presents limitations. Though plastic surgeons attempt to modify physical traits we may have inherited, there are basic limitations that cannot be changed. We have limitations, and we have to learn to live within these restrictions.

Many of us spend a lot of time kicking against these restraints. We are like the child in kindergarten who got tired of playing in a group game. One day the child said to her teacher, "I don't want to do that anymore." The teacher said, "That is fine. You go play over there by yourself." It wasn't too long before the child came back to the teacher and asked, "What can I do now? I don't want to do what I want to do."

We all know that sometimes we attempt to kick against the restraints and discipline in society because we feel that we should have absolute freedom, but absolute freedom is an illusion. We all have to live within certain kinds of limitations. Suppose I had before me a violin string. I am free to do a number of things with the string. I can tie it in a knot. I can attach things to it or stick it in my pocket. But I cannot make it sing until I attach it to the violin, because it is "disciplined" to that instrument if it is to fulfill its purpose. It is not free to do just anything. There is no such thing as absolute freedom.

A Disciplined Life

Paul reminds us that we all have to live a disciplined life. He used the athlete as an illustration. He pictured one who had mastered his body as he ran for the prize in a race. Athletes are usually good examples of those who have disciplined their bodies for various sports. Discipline is a necessary part of authentic living. Without discipline, there is only anarchy. Many enjoy being at football games or watching them on television. If there were no rules and no discipline, there would be no real game of football. If there were no goal posts, no restrictions on how far a player had to run for a first down, or no limit to the number of downs a team needs to have to retain possession of the ball, there would be no game. Without disciplines and rules, there would be no real meaning to the game of football. That is true whether it is baseball, basketball, tennis, a card game, or another sport. Restrictions and discipline make the game what it is.

No one can really learn to play the piano effectively without discipline. No one learns to play any instrument, like those in an orchestra, without the discipline of mental energy, time, and practice. Discipline is giving one's single-minded attention to what one has before them. I am told that if a person wants to play golf effectively and continue to be efficient, there is one basic rule that each player needs to remember. That simple rule is "keep your eye on the ball." If you have been playing golf for a long time, the simple rule is still "keep your eye on the ball." Most major mistakes in golf come from not following that simple rule. So it is with life.

We are challenged to have a singleness of vision. Jesus reminds us, "The eye is the lamp of the body. So, if your eye is sound, your whole body will be full of light" (Matt 6:22). Jesus called us to a singleness of vision. The Apostle Paul said, "This one thing I do" (Phil 3:13). Learn to focus. Learn to direct your life toward a particular cause or purpose—this is discipline. Learn the value of control. With discipline, there is a narrowing of focus. Discipline means you can't do everything. You have to begin to focus your attention in a narrow way. If you are going to accomplish whatever task is before you, you can't be all things in all places. You have to narrow your vision to discover discipline. Athletes become successful in football, basketball, or another sport as they narrow their focus and begin to try to equip themselves to compete in that sport more effectively. Hours on end are given over to practice before this goal can be realized.

It was said that when people watched the famous artist Whistler at work, they were amazed at how quickly he could paint his pictures. But what they did not know was that before he came to his final painting, he sometimes would paint a hundred different pictures until he was finally satisfied that he had captured what he was striving for. All of the earlier pictures were discarded until he finally came to the one that satisfied him. This cost him time, discipline, and energy.

When Fritz Kreisler, the famous violinist, began his study of the violin, he was not sure that it was what he wanted to do at all. He came to our country at age fourteen and had a tour with only modest reception. On returning to his home country of Austria, he could not even make the second violinist in the Philharmonic. He then gave up the violin for a while. He tried medicine, but he did not like it. He tried painting, but that was not satisfying. He even turned to the military but was not happy with that. He finally decided that he would take up the violin again—but this time he decided to study it seriously. For the first eight weeks after he took up the instrument again, he did nothing but finger exercises. This time when he began to play the violin, he noticed in himself a big difference. From then on, day after day, week after week, and year after year, he disciplined himself to perfecting the instrument. After a performance many years later, a woman came up to him and said, "Oh, I would give my life if I could play like you do." He replied gently, "Madam, I did." He gave his life that he might master that instrument.

Discipline Provides Focus

Discipline is learning to focus one's life in a narrow way to gain control over a particular area. This comes about only at the cost of time, effort, and energy. With discipline comes accountability, responsibility, and stewardship. Any person who seeks to discipline their life has to have responsibility and accountability for whatever kind of action they take. All freedom is a trust we have to use or abuse, waste or share, conserve or destroy. Of those to whom much has been given, much is required in the stewardship of our lives. Yes, we have freedom, but that freedom sounds an accountability alarm within our minds. Martin Luther said, "Love God and do as you please." Note, though, that freedom is conditioned first on the freedom to love God. When we truly love God, then we will desire for our lives what God desires.

An old parable seems appropriate for this subject. A chicken and pig were walking down the road. They saw a sign by the side of the road: "Help a Needy Family." The chicken looked over at the pig and said, "You know, we could help a needy family." "How?" asked the pig. "We could give them a breakfast of ham and eggs," the chicken replied. The pig thought on that for a while. "Yes," he exclaimed. "We could. But from you, chicken, it would only require a contribution. But from me total commitment." In life we have to learn that commitments are required of us. Too many of us want to give token contributions, so we never really become disciplined. We cannot have a sense of direction and guidance until we have mastered our bodies as Paul wrote about in 1 Corinthians 9.

The Christian Goal in Life

Notice also that Paul reminds his readers that the athlete runs toward a goal. The reason you master your body and the reason you commit yourself to discipline is to achieve the goal before you. Paul said that many of the runners ran for a prize that would fade away and soon be gone. The Christian, though, runs for a prize that is everlasting. Through the redemption that God gives us through Christ, we share in life eternal. I suppose one of the saddest things is to see people who are busy going but who have no direction. They are busy moving through life without purpose. Our lives cry out for direction, meaning, and purpose. Why are we going where we are going? What is the purpose of our going? The Apostle Paul reminds us that the Christ-like life makes all the difference. Christ is the one who gives us our direction and goal for living.

Jesus proclaimed that he had come to bring "deliverance to the captives" (Luke 4:18). He came to set free those who were in bondage. He came to set them free from their slavery to tradition. He came to deliver captives from their blindness, pain, disease, deafness, and sin. He sought to give life. Jesus said, "You shall know the truth and the truth will set you free" (John 8:32). Christ himself became the truth. He gave us the way to life, and he filled it with purpose and meaning. When you and I harness our life with his, then we find that he gives us the strength, guidance, direction, and goal to walk in a meaningful way. We then strive to live in accord with the Christ-like way of grace and love.

It is sad when people think Christ comes into a life to be destructive or harmful. Lance Webb tells a modified version of the parable of the lost sheep. One day a little sheep wanders off from the rest of the flock. He discovers some rich green grass and enjoys feeding on it. Before he knows it, he moves into a thicket and becomes entangled in the briars. After a while he realizes he is lost, and he looks up and sees the wolf coming. He is terrified. He begins to run with all his effort to escape the wolf until he comes to a cliff. He looks over a high precipice and knows that he either has to leap to his death or face the wolf. As he turns around to face the wolf, he discovers that it is not the wolf at all, but it is the sheepdog who has come to take him back home.[1]

Too many of us wander into wildernesses. We, like the prodigal son, go off and we think that the God who is pursuing us—the

"Hound of Heaven," in poet Francis Thompson's words—is coming to destroy us. But God is coming to give us life, to give us direction, to give us purpose, to give us redemption, to give us wholeness in order that we can be a full, complete person. When we commit our lives to him, we find that life is not destructive but constructive. Life is not without meaning. Christ gives us the real purpose for our existence.

Discipline Is Not Easy

But note this: In no way does the Apostle Paul tell us that discipline is always easy. He says he mastered his body like an athlete does for endurance and skill. "I pommel my body" literally translates "to deliver a blow to the eye." He gave himself a black eye. The imagery is that of a boxer who has undergone the rigid discipline of an athlete to bring his body under control and up to its best strength. This is costly and difficult. Paul at no time said that the Christian way was easy. He put himself under the necessary discipline. He was willing to suffer persecution, rejection, ridicule, and imprisonment for Christ. Jesus himself told us that the gospel had a sandpaper edge to it, and those who followed him would sometimes find that his way was hard and difficult. But even along that difficult way, it gives us the abundant life.

Out of the transformation Christ brings in our lives, we discover who we are as authentic people. All things must be brought under some kind of discipline before their potential can be realized. Coal buried under the earth's surface doesn't serve any purpose until it is dug up and disciplined for heat. Oil and gas within the earth are not of much value until they are brought up from their depths and given new direction, discipline, and guidance. Water flowing down a stream is not helpful as a source of power until a dam is constructed to harness the water's energy and convert it into electricity. It must first be disciplined. All life requires discipline. As we relate to the God of the universe, we find real meaning. But that doesn't mean God's way is always easy. Those who proclaim that anyone who follows Jesus Christ will become wealthy or find an easy way in life have not read the New Testament very carefully. In no place does Jesus promise his followers that kind of life. Paul did not make that kind of promise either, and he certainly did not live that kind of life.

Several years ago, a minister was talking with one of his church members who had been in the Coast Guard in the Second World War. The man told the minister about an experience during the war when four American patrol boats had an assignment in the waters around Greenland. They were caught in a fierce Arctic storm. It was a freezing, stormy day. Three of the ships had moved up close to the shore, and ice froze on the decks, masts, and gear. They fought against it, but the three ships became so laden with ice that they finally sank. The captain of the fourth patrol boat was an experienced Norwegian who knew the waters well. He turned his ship and headed out into the fury of the storm. The others could not believe it. But in the midst of the storm, away from the shore, the winds were so fierce, the rains were lighter, and the waves were so forceful that ice hardly had time to form on the ship. This captain's ship was spared because he was knew how to and was willing to turn into the storm. By going into the storm and difficulty, his ship and crew were spared. The harder way enabled him to survive. God's way may look like the harder way, but it really is the way that brings us redemption, meaning, and abundant life.

Today many people are enslaved by bad habits like alcohol, drugs, or lust. Others are enslaved by selfish ambitions in their goals and purposes for life. Still others are enslaved by fears of all kinds— illness, loss of job, or death. Some suffer from depression, loneliness, anxiety, and helplessness and may need medical intervention or counseling. We need to let Jesus Christ come into our lives to give us real freedom. We can make a choice in life to be enslaved by lesser forces or to commit ourselves in bondage to Christ. Real freedom in life is deciding which Master we will allow to control us. Choosing not to choose Christ is still a choice. Freedom is not living an undisciplined life. Real freedom is being controlled by a Master who is worthy of our loyalty. Paul found his freedom when he was in bondage to Christ. When Christ makes us free, we are free indeed.

Chapter 7

Women in Ministry
1 Corinthians 11:2-16

Here is an old riddle. A father and his son are riding in their automobile. The car swerves off the road and crashes into a tree. When the rescue squad gets there, they discover that the father is already dead, and the son is seriously injured. The ambulance takes him to the hospital, and the doctor looks at the young boy and exclaims, "My God, it's my son!" In decades past, people wondered "How can it be?" Why, of course, the doctor is a woman! Thankfully fewer people are stymied by this riddle than they once were.

Leo Tolstoy wrote this comment a number of years ago: "I am only going to tell the truth about women when I am standing with one foot in the grave. I shall say it, jump into the coffin, pull the lid shut, and then say, 'do with me as you want.'" Professor Higgins, in *My Fair Lady*, asks as he sings, "Why can't a woman be more like a man?" Today there are some folks who say, "Well, they sure are trying to be more like men." But maybe within the church the better question is, "Why are men and women not more like Christ?"

Now I have the audacity, with some timidity, to approach the subject of the role of women in ministry. Obviously, this is just a beginning statement, because no one can address this issue fully in a few pages. But I shall attempt to share some things I have found from my studies of the Scriptures and other writings that have been helpful to me. Several years ago, I preached a sermon challenging the resolution from the Southern Baptist Convention stating that women are considered to be the primary cause of the fall of civilization. The SBC statement asserted that that sin came into the world because of Eve.[1] A few proof-texts were quoted that overlooked Paul's great epistle to the Romans in which he placed the blame for sin clearly on Adam. It also overlooked the whole Christian concept of grace. Grace, not sin, is the primary ingredient in the Christian's life now.

Avoid Using an Isolated Scripture as the Whole Truth

Our denominations and churches and individual Bible studies need to be careful never to take one isolated passage of Scripture and assume that it contains the whole of God's revelation. We need to find the truth within a particular passage and incorporate it into the greater truth of the whole of Scripture. We must also remember that sometimes a Scripture passage may be concerned with a particular situation or problem from the time in which it was written and may not be a teaching meant for our day. One quick example: I have observed that very few people in most of our congregations have taken seriously Jesus's lesson to the rich young ruler: "Go and sell everything you have and come follow me" (Luke 18:22). Most of us assume that this teaching was meant for that man in that particular place. Neither you nor I, nor most others, have taken those particular words as being directed toward us.

Women in Ancient Israel

Where do we begin to try to get a handle on this issue? Let's start by seeing how women were perceived in the ancient history of Israel. Women did not have many rights. They did not have an identity primarily as individuals; their identity came from being part of a family. They lived in a patriarchal system in which a widow without children was expected to remain with her husband's family in hopes that one of his brothers would marry her according to the Levitical practice, and she would bear children for her dead husband through this brother. At the death of the husband, his property passed to his sons first, and if there were no sons, it went to the daughters. None of the inheritance would go to the widow upon the husband's death. It went first to his male relatives on his father's side. When a man listed his property, he would include his wife as part of the property.

A man could divorce his wife, but a woman could not divorce her husband. A man could ask a woman to prove her virginity before he would marry her, and after they were married, at any time in his life, whether he was in a jealous rage or whatever, he could demand that she prove if she had been faithful to him by submitting to various tests. But she could never ask the same of him.

A Jewish man would pray every morning: "Praise be God that he has not created me a Gentile. Praise be God that he has not created me a woman. Praise be God that he has not created me a slave or an ignorant man." This prayer clearly reflects the social attitude toward women in the Jesus's day. There is no question that women were placed on a different level altogether in ancient Jewish history.

Women as Exceptions in God's Service

Look, however, at some interesting exceptions. There are examples of women who were called by God and who served in powerful ways in ancient Israel. For example, Miriam, the sister of Moses, was called a prophet of God (Exod 15:20-25). The prophet Micah stated that God used Moses, Aaron, and Miriam to lead Israel out of Egypt into freedom (Mic 6:3-4). Deborah was a judge with authority who could summon a man, Barak, to come at her command, and he would come. She was also a prophet and went with Barak to support him in battle because he was afraid to go without her. She was a decisive leader who brought Israel peace for forty years (Judg 4:1-10). There were other exceptions, such as Huldah, mentioned in 2 Kings 22:14-20, who was a prophet to Josiah the king in the seventh century BC. Josiah followed her advice in many of his national reforms. Noadiah (Neh 6:14) and the wife of Isaiah (Isa 8:3) were also prophets. Esther the queen is remembered for her strong defense of the Jews in their time of national danger. Joel said that one day both young men and young women shall prophesy (Joel 2:28). So even in ancient Israel women were occasionally prophets, speaking for God, and some were rulers too.

Jesus's Relationship to Women

With the coming of Jesus, the scene began to change. Some may wonder, "If God wanted to change the situation for women, why did God not come as a woman instead of as a man?" Even as a man, Jesus was often rejected and eventually killed on a cross. If God had come incarnate as a woman in the first century, with their male-dominated traditions and customs, there is no way she would have been accepted as the Messiah. But notice what the man Jesus Christ did for women in his ministry. In the listings of followers of Jesus, women are always mentioned as being among Jesus's disciples (Matt 27:55). They often helped with money and financed his ministry as Jesus traveled around Palestine (Luke 8:2-3). Jesus taught women directly, which was in violation of the rabbinic tradition of his day. Women, it was believed, could not possibly understand the Torah (see Luke 8:1-3). But Jesus went into the home of Mary and Martha and taught them (Luke 10:38-42). He taught the woman at the well, who was also a Samaritan, enemy to Jews of that day (John 4:1-42). Jesus not only talked with women but also made physical contact with them. Ordinarily, a man in Jesus's day would not even let a woman count money into his hand because she might touch him and thus defile him in public. Jesus reached out to a woman who had been crippled for eighteen years, touched her, and called her a daughter of Abraham (Luke 13:10-13). He enabled her to stand upright with dignity and defended her from his critics (13:14-17).

Jesus constantly broke all kinds of traditions. He touched women in need. He touched the outcasts of society—the blind, deaf, lepers, and sinners. By doing so, he broke through all kinds of oppressive traditions. Jesus accepted the anointing of his feet by a woman who let her hair down in public, which was considered a disgraceful act. As a rabbi, he knew this gesture was forbidden, yet he felt no sense of outrage but accepted it and used it as a prophetic word about his own death (John 12:1-8). I could list many other occasions, but probably one of the most powerful proofs of Jesus's value of women is that all four Gospels record that the resurrected Christ appeared to women first. It is interesting that in 1 Corinthians where Paul writes about the resurrection appearances of Jesus, no women are listed—only men. But all four Gospels tell us that Jesus Christ appeared first to women. Why did Paul not list these women? It is possible that he hid this fact in order to be seen as valid. In that day, a woman legally could not be a witness. Her word was not accepted as legal evidence. Nevertheless, Jesus appeared first to women after the resurrection.

A Look at Paul's Attitude

Paul's writings bring up several questions about women. What are we to say about the strange passage from 1 Corinthians 11? Some people are quick to say that Paul was probably a male chauvinist. Others say that some of the statements he makes in this epistle are a clear indication that he never married. How do we deal with his words? In some Bible translations, a heading might be put on this section that reads, "The proper dress of women in church" or "Head covering for church." Paul seems to be concerned with personal and local problems in the church at Corinth. As he wrestles with these problems, he seems to shift from one foot to the other trying to see how he can say something constructive to the people. He is not writing about veils like a woman might wear over her face but about a head covering. In that day, it was a disgrace for a woman not to have a head covering in public because she would be considered morally loose. If she wore her hair hanging down without a covering, people might think of her as a woman of ill repute. She might even be mistaken for one of the temple prostitutes of the many false gods worshiped in Corinth. Because of these views, Paul encouraged women to wear their hair up so they would not be mistaken for prostitutes. They would also be following the tradition for a woman's dress in that day and age.

Proper Dress

Paul's concern here, however, is not merely about the way women ought to dress in church; he is also addressing how men ought to dress in church. The basic conclusion he reaches seems to be that women ought to dress like women and look like women, and men ought to dress like men and look like men. It seems that the basic problem underlying Paul's words here is the fear of homosexuality. If improper dress was worn in Christian worship, men might be mistaken for women and women for men. Paul wanted the church to avoid any hint of homosexuality in the appearance of its members. He argued that each person should be distinctive in their sexual dress. Is the primary issue about women not cutting their hair and men not wearing theirs long? Is the issue about women always wearing hats? I don't think so. The real issue seems to be not external appearance but a deeper problem. Paul's hidden agenda seems to be this: "Let neither men nor women lose their sexual distinctions. Let no questions arise about who you are as a person! Let a man wear his hair like a man and a woman wear hers like a woman."[2]

God as Source

When Paul finally reaches his conclusion on this matter, it is not that man is superior to woman because he was created first. The use of the word "head" or "source" here is like the reference to the origin of a river. What is its source? In a hierarchical order, all creation owes its origin to God. Man's source is Christ. Woman's source is man. The source of Christ is God. Rather than proving that woman is subordinate to man, Paul is arguing that man is not independent of woman nor woman of man. Woman was made from man, but man is now born of woman, and all things come from God. He is saying that man is as dependent on woman as woman is on man, because he does not have life without her, and ultimately both are dependent on God. God is the Creator. God is the source of life. We come from God.

God did not desire men and women to be indistinguishable. If this had been God's goal, God would have made them that way in the creative process. To the Corinthians, Paul states that their sexual differences should be obvious. The phrase about wearing the veil "for the sake of the angels" was probably a reference to the giving of the law (Gal 3:19) where the woman wore her veil as a sign of her husband's authority over her in ancient Jewish tradition. Now a woman has authority to fill a position in worship that was denied to her before the coming of Christ. Christ set women as well as men free from the law.

On Being Silent in Church

Those who want to flip to 1 Corinthians 14 (vv. 34-35), where Paul talks about women being silent in church, must take the fifth verse of this chapter into account where he indicates that "all of you"—including women and men—are both praying and prophesying (preaching) in the church. Prophesying is "forth-telling," not "fore-telling," and it is like preaching today. What are we to do with the passage where Paul states that women are to be silent in church? It should be obvious that then, like now, women were not always silent in church. They were speaking privately and publicly, because Paul said that they were both praying and preaching (11:5). Usually, the early church met in the large homes of various people. Would we say to a woman like Lydia, who held church meetings in her own home, "Be quiet; you can't talk here. This is no longer your home"?

I think this was a local problem that Paul was trying to deal with in his own day. The issue had caused a disturbance in the local church. Remember that women, who had not been allowed to worship with men before this time, were now suddenly coming into a service of worship where they all worshiped together. In the Jewish temple there was a court for the Gentiles, a court for women, and then, closest to the holiest part of the temple, a court for the men. Women were now coming into the worship services with men, and so perhaps they were talking with each other and with the men and asking questions about the service. Paul may have been saying, in essence, "Don't talk all the time while somebody else is talking. Be quiet." I do not think that this is a pronouncement that woman should never be permitted to speak in church. Paul is staying to stop the chatter at the wrong times. At other times, he also tells the men to stop chattering. All of this is also set against another problem in the church—the prevalence of glossolalia or speaking in tongues. Those who "spoke in tongues" might jump up without any notice and begin to speak. Paul's main concern seemed to be more with order and not with an attempt to control the Spirit.

On Trying to Take this Passage Literally

I am not convinced that these are indeed Paul's words. It is interesting to me that those who take literally the passage of Scripture stating that a woman should keep silent in church do not acknowledge that it was directed to a local situation. It is also interesting to me that these people try to make that passage a universal truth, but they do not take literally the passages stating that a woman should not cut her hair or have her head uncovered in worship. In another place, Paul condemns the wearing of jewelry, but few have taken that literally.

Many scholars interpret 1 Corinthians 14:33-35 as an interpolation because it interrupts the theme of prophecy, and it is different in linguistic usage from the rest of Paul's letter.[3] Some see it as a "marginal gloss" written in the margin of the manuscript and inserted in the text later by a reader to conform to his own worship practices. This insertion not only interrupts the flow of Paul's argument but also contradicts what Paul writes in many other places.[4] Even if one tries to take this passage literally, which I don't, the truth is that Paul was dealing with contemporary problems here that were not meant to be universal truths for future generations.

All Are One in Christ Jesus

Paul's universal truth was that in Christ there is no male nor female, no Greek or Jew, no slave or free. In Christ we are all one (Gal 3:28). In this great truth, he asserts what has happened by the power of Jesus Christ our Lord. Sometimes Paul was willing to compromise slightly his ideal goal that the gospel might be proclaimed effectively to people who were tied to customs and traditions. He did not think circumcision amounted to anything when one was in Christ, yet he agreed to have Timothy circumcised rather than have the Jerusalem Jewish Christians upset and the Christian cause endangered (Acts 16:3). He asked Onesimus, the runaway slave, to come back to his master and be faithful to him, because these social customs could not be changed immediately (Philemon). Even Jesus himself noted that the ideal of marriage where man and woman should never divorce was softened by Moses because of the hardening of people's hearts

(Matt 19). Paul had his ideal, and he challenged the early Christians to move beyond much of their cultural influences, but he also was willing to bend so that the greater, more valuable truth might become a reality. As Christians, we are challenged to recognize the truth that was intended for Paul's time and to discover the greater truth that we can apply today.

Women Who Followed Christ

Look for a moment at some truths we can pull from these Scriptures for our lives today. The first is that Jesus Christ has given to us a new humanity. There is no male or female within his kingdom. As I mentioned earlier, Jesus Christ reached out to women in all walks of life, and they were also among his followers. Women's lives were changed by Jesus. Jesus treated women as authentic people who have needs just like men. Many examples come to mind: the woman at the well (John 4:1-42), the woman taken in the act of adultery (John 7:53–8:11), a sick woman who touched his garment (Mark 5:24-34), a Canaanite woman (Matt 15:21-28), Mary and Martha (Luke 10:38-42; John 11:1-44), the sinful woman who anointed Jesus (Luke 7:36-50), and countless other women. The Gospels also bear witness that it was the women around Jesus who remained nearby at his trial and crucifixion, and Mary Magdalene, also a woman, was the first to witness the risen Christ. Richard Rohr argues that because Mary was a witness to the resurrected Christ, she was indeed an apostle. The definition of an apostle was one who had witnessed the resurrection. So she was an apostle! Rohr says that the argument that only males could be admitted to the priesthood is undone by her being the first witness to the resurrection, which makes her an apostle.[5] Jesus accepted women into his kingdom because he had come to make a new covenant, a new Israel, and a new humanity. God had created humanity originally as male and female, and in God's new kingdom their oneness is emphasized anew. Men and women are part of the one family of God.

Women in the Early Church

After the ascension of Jesus, the New Testament notes that women were a vital part of the early church. They were a part of the praying community (Acts 1:14). Women as well as men received the Holy Spirit and the gift of tongues (Acts 2:1-4). Women were included among the first converts to Christ (Acts 5:14). The first European convert was a wealthy woman named Lydia (Acts 16:14-15). In many places, women are listed as coworkers in spreading the gospel: Prisca and Claudia (2 Tim 4:19, 21); Mary, Persis, Tryphaena, and Tryphosa (Rom 16:6, 12); Dorcas (Acts 9:36-42); Euodia and Syntyche (Phil 4:2-3). Junia was called prominent among the apostles (Rom 16:7 NRSV). At the conclusion to his Roman letter, Paul expresses greetings to twenty-eight people. Ten of these are women who helped spread the gospel. Phoebe is listed as a deacon in the church at Cenchreae (Rom 16:1-2). The Greek word for *deacon* here is the same word that is used every other place when it is listed with a man's name. In those places, it is clearly rendered "deacon" or "minister." And with Phoebe's name, it should be the same. She was not only a deacon in the church but is referred to as a ruler over many, including Paul.

Priscilla (or Prisca), the wife of Aquila, is mentioned six times. She is listed as a teacher of Apollos, who became one of the great preachers in New Testament times (Acts 18:24-26; see also Rom 16:3-5; 2 Tim 4:19; Acts 18:18-19). Timothy had been taught the faith by women—his mother Eunice and grandmother Lois (2 Tim 1:5). The early church often met in the houses of women: Lydia (Acts 16:14-15), Nympha (Col 4:15), and Priscilla and Aquila (Rom 16:3, 5; 1 Cor 16:19). After Paul had a vision in Troas one night of a man calling him to come to Macedonia and help, Paul went there and ended up by a river in Philippi, where he met with a group of women praying. Lydia and her household were converted there. Note, as mentioned earlier, that this first convert in Europe was not a man but a woman (Acts 16:9-15).[6]

Jesus Removed the Wall Between the Sexes

Jesus removed the dividing wall between people. When the veil in the temple was torn in two at his death (Matt 27:51), it was symbolic not only of the closer relationship that each person could have with God but also of the closer relationship each person could have with another, whether male or female. Jesus broke down the dividing wall so we can come closer to God and have a more meaningful relationship with God. We are not separated from God because of our sex, race, or age. Jesus was the great liberator. He removed the walls that enclosed the poor, lame, blind, deaf, ill, those in bondage, women, the aged, children, sinners, and others. He opened the door to freedom.

In *Children's Letters to God*, a young girl writes, "Dear God, Are boys better than girls? I know that you are one but try to be fair." Several years ago, I wrote an article for a church magazine and asked the question, "Is God Male or Female?" The immediate answer for most of us is that God is masculine, especially since we pray, "Our Father." But surely God is not just male because that limits God to our human terms. God is all that constitutes masculinity, yes, but God is also all that constitutes the essence of womanhood. God is spirit. God is beyond sexual distinction and not limited by it. Jesus said that there is no marriage in heaven (Matt 22:30). We will be like the angels. God is beyond sexual distinction. We say "Father" because God is personal, but God is not a person. God is above all and loves us with divine grace and has shattered all dividing walls to draw us close to God's self and to one another.

Women as Genuine People

In order for God's kingdom to reign on earth, women need to be seen as people, not just extensions of men. They do not find their fulfillment in life merely through somebody else. A woman is uniquely who she is as a person before God. Because God loved her and created her as a person, she should have the opportunity to be recognized as the authentic person she is with her own gifts. Each woman is a human being of worth in and of her own right. Whether or not she is married or a mother, she is still a person of great worth, and she has love and purpose in the sight of God. Surely this should be true in the eyes of the church.

The Gifts of Women in Ministry

Women have their own great gifts to contribute in ministry, and they need opportunities to utilize these gifts. We should not try to restrict them to one type of service reserved only for women. Do we confine a woman to the church nursery or kitchen? Do we forbid her opportunities to minister in roles that often have been seen as reserved for men? When you say to a woman, "You have to be silent in church," that means, if taken literally, she can't sing or be in the church choir. She could not be permitted to sing a solo, pray, read Scripture, give a testimony, or teach a Sunday school class. Do you hear the hypocrisy of some who say women should be silent in church and still let her do these things but don't permit her to speak or preach in worship? Some will say that there is only one thing she really can't do, and that is preach. Who says so?

We have clear evidence within the Scriptures that women were preaching in New Testament times, and there were also prophets in the Old Testament days. If we are to be honest in our faith, we can't use one isolated verse of Scripture to condemn women for responding to the call of God as they hear it. When I was teaching homiletics at seminary, it was often interesting to me that in some of my classes, women were often the most gifted preachers. I and others recognized their gifts but knew that they might have a difficult road in finding a place of service in Baptist churches.

Women Still Find Restrictions in Ministry

Still today, we need to acknowledge that it may not be easy for women to find their rightful place in ministry, because even in the church of Jesus Christ, where all the walls are supposed to have fallen down and where sexual roles should be on the same level, there is still prejudice, tradition, and customs that many cannot overcome. We know the road has been uphill and it will not always be easy, but that doesn't

mean we as Christians should not attempt to improve it and incorporate within our own congregation a pattern closer to authentic New
Testament Christianity. We have also witnessed today that women
have been called to some of the most distinguished preaching and
religious leadership posts in our country—Amy Butler to Riverside
Church as pastor in New York City, Susan Sparks to Madison Avenue
Baptist Church in New York City, Serene Jones as president of Union
Theological Seminary in New York, Molly Marshall as president
of Central Baptist Theological Seminary, Leonora Tubbs Tisdale
as professor of preaching at Princeton Theological Seminary, Amy
Starr Redwine as pastor of First Presbyterian Church in Richmond,
Virginia, and Julia Pennington Russell as pastor of First Baptist
Church in Washington, D.C. Many other gifted women serve as
pastors of small churches in cities and in the country and on the staff
of large churches in many areas today. Women have teaching posts
in the biblical areas in many seminaries and universities. In many of
our churches, women serve as leaders in a variety of roles, as deacons
and chairpersons of committees and boards. Their gifts are acknowledged, affirmed, and utilized. We can be grateful for the progress and
still understand that we can do better.

A number of years ago, in another church I once served, I had the
two Sunday sermon subjects listed on the exterior bulletin board. For
Sunday morning it read, "Woman's Liberation: You've Come a Long
Way, Baby." Sunday night's title was "I Have Washed My Hands of
That." The evening sermon didn't have anything to do with the other,
and I was sorry the titles ended up together on the bulletin board.
The contradiction between them distracted from what I was trying to
say to affirm women in ministry. There are a lot of people, however,
who want to wash their hands of women who want their rights, or
they prefer to make jokes about the issue or try to stand in women's
way when they want to serve as ministers. This is a serious issue that
should concern the whole church. Jesus Christ died for all of us, and
he came so all believers might have their full place in grace and in
ministry and in service for him.

The Ministry of Women Is Essential

We need to affirm that the ministry of women is essential to the ongoing ministry of the church. Women were utterly indispensable in the New Testament church, and that is also true today. What would the church be without the role of women in its ministry? This is true whether they are ordained or not. Let each serve in her place in the church as God leads her to minister. There are many needs in the church, and the responsibilities of leadership and decision-making can be shared by men and women in a great variety of ways. Without the ministry of women, many of today's local churches would be dead. Judith Bailey states in her book *Strength for the Journey: Feminist Theology & Baptist Women Pastors* that one of the goals of feminist theologians is that women be included in all aspects of worship, including preaching and using inclusive language in Scripture, hymns, readings, and prayers.[7] This should be the goal of all our churches today. The role of women is essential in ministry today.

All People Are Called to Be Servants

Women, like men, in whatever role they have within the church, are called to be servants—not masters, not lords. All of us, whether we are male or female, are called to serve. I hope that in the church, as we attempt to listen to the guidance of God, we shall invite women who have gifts in administration to administrate. Invite women who have gifts in teaching to teach. Invite women who have gifts in music to be involved with us in our music. Invite women who have gifts in counseling to counsel. Invite women who have gifts in preaching to preach. May we utilize whatever gifts women have to the glory of God. Let us bless them as they respond to God's leadership in their lives. Their path will not be easy, but it will be in keeping with Christ.

So today, I say to women, join your hands with Miriam, Deborah, Mary, Lydia, Phoebe, Elizabeth Hooten, Lucretia Mott, Anna Howard Shaw, Antionette Brown Blackwell, Lottie Moon, Georgia Harkness, Elizabeth Achtemeier, Phyllis Trible, Elizabeth O'Connor, Karen Armstrong, Pheme Perkins, Diana Butler Bass,

Barbara Brown Taylor, Amy Butler, Eboni Marshall Turman, Molly Marshall, Phyllis Rodgerson Pleasants Tessieri, Linda McKinnish Bridges, Jana Childers, Mary Donovan Turner, and all the other women down through history who have linked their lives in ministry for Jesus Christ as Lord. Find your place of service. Seek to utilize your gifts for him. Do it with grace, dignity, compassion, and love. And those of us who are men, let us find ways to support women so they may discover their role in ministry. Whatever your gift is in ministry within your church, use it faithfully and well. May we all hear Christ say to each of us, "When I set you free, you are free indeed."

Chapter 8

The Last Supper Received from the Lord

1 Corinthians 11:17-34

Paul received word that the church at Corinth was abusing the Lord's Supper. Some of the wealthy members of the congregation arrived early and ate most of the food provided for the meal, and others consumed wine until they became drunk. This behavior offended those who arrived later, like the poor or slaves, who then had little to eat, and they felt humiliated from the contempt shown in the attitude of the rich. They were supposed to be gathering to observe the Lord's Supper. In these verses, Paul reminds the young church of the proper approach to this sacred meal.

The Setting for the Lord's Supper

Paul reminds the Corinthians that the Lord's Supper was first observed on the last night Jesus took the Passover meal with his disciples—the night when Judas later betrayed him. Paul indicates that his description of the observation of the meal is information he "received from the Lord" (1 Cor 11:23). He notes that Jesus picked up the loaf of bread, gave thanks, and told his disciples, "This is my body which is for you. Do this in remembrance of me" (vv. 23-24). The broken bread pointed them to the sacrifice that Jesus would make later on the cross with his broken body. Now, this bread summons believers like the Corinthians not to forget that sacrifice made by the one who is "the bread of life."

The Bread of Life

When Jesus said, "I am the bread of life" (John 6:35), his listeners probably first thought about their own physical hunger. Bread is essential to sustain life. In a real sense, life depends on bread. It comes from outside of us and provides nourishment and strength. Bread is a symbol of our complete dependence on God. It is the sustenance we must have to live. God is concerned with our physical hungers, and Jesus taught us to pray for our "daily bread." Our physical needs are important to God, and God is certainly concerned about the hungry people of the world. We have seen the swollen stomachs, gaunt faces and bodies of the world's hungriest people. You and I have probably never known true hunger in our lives. God has challenged us to help meet the needs of those who do.

In Jesus's words, "I am the bread of life," he is speaking about more than physical hunger. When he made this declaration, he was saying that he provides food for our deepest longings and hungers. He declared that he alone will satisfy the needs, wants, and hungers of humanity with his own presence. People do not live by bread alone. Christ fulfills the hungers of the human heart.

Jesus says, "I am the bread of life." We cannot separate what Christ gives from who he is. They are linked together. We cannot take the teachings of Jesus apart from the man/Christ, the Son of God. They are interwoven. "I am the bread of life." Jesus is at the center of his teachings. In the Gospel of John Jesus also says, "For the bread of God is that which comes down from heaven and gives life to the world" (John 6:33). Christ is the one who has come to us from God. He is God's gift to us. He is the Incarnate One. He is not just any man; he is "the man." He is the bread from above—the one through whom God has revealed God's self in the highest and fullest sense.

Reminders from this Meal

This passage is Paul's reminder to the Corinthians as they gather at the Lord's Table. He reminds them and us that we need to receive this bread in memory of what Jesus did. We also need to note that we have to feed upon the bread of life if we are to be nourished. Our physical bodies cannot be strengthened if we never eat food. In a similar way, for our spiritual bodies to be sustained, Christ must be assimilated and incorporated into our lives. We draw him into our being through trust and faith. If we really believe that Jesus Christ is Lord and Savior, then we must trust him. We must draw him into our lives. We must open our hearts and let him come in, nourish, and feed us.

Having opened our lives to him and experienced his entrance into our lives, we need continuously to remain open to him. Life in Christ is not merely a onetime event. As we go back to the table to be nourished again and again with physical food, so we come back to Christ to be fed again and again that we might continue to grow and be sustained by him. Spiritual development is not accomplished by meeting Christ just once. The new birth is the beginning point of salvation, and then spiritual growth and development takes place as we are constantly nourished and fortified by him.

When Jesus said, "I am the bread of life," he also declared "that a man may eat of it and not die" (John 6:50). We want to ask Jesus, "What do you mean when you say that we will never die?" The disciples died physically, didn't they? But we really do not understand Jesus's offer when we associate it only with our earthly lives. Physical food is essential for our lives to be sustained in this world. But the food Jesus gives us is eternal food. It nourishes our inner being, our soul. It fortifies the spiritual person so that we may have life eternal through Christ. It is food that lasts because our souls are nourished and fed by him.

When Jesus said, "I am the bread of life," it was a divine claim. On the front of the Communion table in St. Matthews Baptist Church, where I served as pastor for ten years, stalks of grain are carved. The carvings remind us that Christ is the bread of life, the one who feeds, nourishes, and sustains us.

The Vine of Life

On this same Communion table, the figure of the vine is also carved. Remember that the grape juice or wine in the cup comes from the

grapes off the grapevine. In the fifteenth chapter of the Gospel of
John, Jesus makes this bold declaration: "I am the true vine. I am
the real vine." Jesus knew that the children of Israel understood
something about vines. They were everywhere. Vineyards dotted the
landscape. Sometimes people would attempt to grow grapes even on
the smallest plot of land. It was the major livelihood in Israel. The
image of the vine was also a part of the heritage of Israel. When
a worshiper approached the synagogue, a carving of the vine was
visible over the doorway. According to Josephus, the great Jewish
historian, there was a massive gold carving of the vine on the temple
in Jerusalem. The carving was so enormous that worshipers were often
absorbed by the splendor of it. The vine, first of all, was symbolic of
the nation Israel. Isaiah depicted Israel as a vine (Isa 5:1-7). Jeremiah
wrote about Israel as the vine of God that had gone wild and turned
away from its original purpose (Jer 2:21).

When Jesus made the declaration, "I am the real vine," this was
a messianic claim. He shattered the Jewish concepts of the destiny of
Israel. "I am the one," Jesus said, "who fulfills your hopes and longing
for the Messiah." Jesus's assertion to be the true vine is a claim to be
the Messiah. Jesus made that claim right after he observed the Last
Supper with his disciples. He and the disciples broke bread together
and shared the cup. Then they walked toward the Mount of Olives;
they may have passed a vineyard where Jesus pointed to the vines and
drew on their symbolism, declaring, "You see those vines. They are
symbolic of the nation Israel, but I am the real vine." It was a startling
declaration. Our life receives true life as we remain united with him.
Jesus Christ is the life-giving stem, and his disciples are the branches.
You and I apart from him do not have real life. As we are united in
him, we have life. As the bread sustains us by our feeding on it, so the
vine nourishes us as we are connected to it. If we are severed from the
vine, then we are cut off from our source of life. I am told that some
grapevines are cut back to the stump until almost nothing is left. But
the vineyard growers know that the branches will come back. No
matter how low you cut them, the vines will grow again.

Sometimes the church seems to be cut back until nothing is left
but a stump. As long as the church is united to Christ, though, there

is life in the branches, and the church can return even when the possibility for growth seems slim. St. Matthews Baptist Church was destroyed by fire. We were cut back to a stump. But from that stump has come new life, new branches, and new growth. From Christ, the church received the power to come back and begin growing again. If we are united in Christ, there is life. Jesus said, "I am the real vine." When we look at the grapes and the vine, let us remember that Christ is the real source of life, and in him you and I find nourishment to sustain us.

Take the Cup

One of the most prominent images on that same Communion table is the chalice or the cup. The cup is an interesting symbol in the Bible. There are many references to the cup. There is "the cup of bitterness," "the cup of agony," and "the cup that overflows," which the writer of the Twenty-third Psalm noted. Salvation from this cup has overflowed and run down through the centuries until you and I can drink of that cup today and find life eternal.

The cup on the Communion table also reminds us of the one Paul mentions here in 1 Corinthians. This is the *cup of the New Covenant*. Jesus shared the Passover meal with his disciples and then lifted his cup to proclaim the beginning of a new era. The cup of blessing was traditionally the last part of this sacred meal. Paul reminds the Corinthians that when Jesus raised high the cup, he declared that this "cup was the New Covenant in my blood. Do this as often as you drink it, in remembrance of me. For as often as you eat this bread and drink the cup, you proclaim the Lord's death until he comes." Jesus had established a new relationship with his disciples. The old Sinai covenant built on the sacrifice of animals was over. Jesus had established a new covenant by his blood. The disciples, who were Jewish, would not literally want to drink blood. Jesus was saying that his death was a sign, a symbol of the outpouring of life and the creation of a new relationship with God. We also are called to share in this meal to remember the sacrifice that Christ made for all of us.

In one of my churches, I remember a member who declined to take Communion one Sunday because she felt she had committed some sins that prevented her from sharing in this sacred meal. The Corinthians were cautioned not to approach the Communion table in an unworthy manner. Would an unproper approach include not coming to the Lord's Table without confessing one's sins, seeking forgiveness, finding pardon, setting relations with others right, accepting others as Christ loved and accepted them, remembering Christ's death and resurrection, and proclaiming thanksgiving for God's love and sacrificial grace? May we approach the table of our Lord remembering his love, sacrifice, death, resurrection, and our sins, accepting God's forgiveness, and boldly declaring our gratitude, love, commitment, and desire to be a vital part of the New Covenant.

Chapter 9

The Spirit at Work in the World

1 Corinthians 2:10-16; 6:19-20; 12:4-13; Acts 2:1-13

In the volume titled *More Children's Letters to God*, a small boy writes, "Dear God, sometimes I think I can see you. I think I saw you last night. Is it a bad thing to say? I would like to very much. My Mommy says you are always near us. Your Friend, Herbert."[1] Like Herbert, you and I at times cry out, "O God, we would like to see you. We would like to touch you, sense you, feel you, and know that you are near us."

How do we know God? How do we sense God? Henry P. van Dusen, in a book written many years ago titled *Spirit, Son and Father*, wrote that "in the faith of the Early Church the Spirit was a central, perhaps the central reality. . . . It sprang directly from vivid, commanding, indubitable experience."[2] It was the Spirit that enabled people to know and see God.

Today the Spirit is not so clearly understood or seen. Our thinking about the Spirit of God has become fuzzy. Some of us cannot begin to comprehend it, or we have trivialized it, sentimentalized it, or ignored it. Many, even within the church, simply do not understand what the Spirit of God is or means. Paul writes in several sections in his letters to the Corinthians about the ministry of the Spirit of God, describing it in different ways.

The Dove

The dove is a prominent figure of the Spirit in the Bible. It is a symbol that the nation of Israel used to express the reality of the presence of God. In Palestine, the dove was viewed as sacred. It could not be hunted or eaten. In the creation story in Genesis 1, God is depicted as a mothering bird hovering and fluttering over the chaos before creation becomes a reality by the divine word. In the story following the flood, a dove is sent out by Noah to search for dry land. The dove returns with a branch that has green leaves, symbolizing that life can begin again. At the baptism of Jesus, a dove descends upon him, signifying that the presence and spirit of God are in him.

The dove has symbolized the Spirit of God in many ways through the centuries. Before the fire that destroyed its sanctuary, St. Matthews Baptist Church in Louisville, Kentucky, where I later served as pastor following the fire, had a descending dove as its central symbol, depicted in the stained-glass window behind the pulpit.

In the Old Testament, Psalm 139:7-12, the writer asks, "Where can I flee from God's presence? Is there someplace I can escape God's Spirit? If I ascend up to the heavens, can I escape God there?" Some have flown to the heavens and literally looked around and declared that they haven't seen God. But God is still there. Even if we ascend to the heights of intellectual brilliance, God is still there, surpassing us. If I descend into Sheol, the place of the dead, God is still there. If I travel to the far seas, the psalmist says, I cannot evade God. To these ancient people, the far seas would have included unknown places, like Japan, China, or America. Even in unknown places, God is still present. If I descend to the realm of darkness and experience the despondency of drugs and alcoholism in the pit, God is still there undergirding me. God's presence is ever present. The fluttering dove-like presence of God's mothering concern is always around us and sustaining us. The dove is a symbol for the inescapable nearness of the presence and power of God.

The Wind

God's presence comes through two powerful symbols in the story in Acts 2. One of these symbols is hard to depict. It is the wind. The Spirit of God is "like wind." It is not wind, but it seems like wind. It makes an audible sound as it comes rushing upon the followers of Christ. God has often been depicted as breath. The Greek word *ruach*, spirit, is feminine and comes from the Greek word *pneuma*, which means "breath" and has a feminine article. That's the reason some scholars project that the Holy Spirit is the feminine side of God. "The feminine pronoun is not as important to all of them (theologians) as it is to me," Barbara Brown Taylor writes, "but the idea of divine multiplicity is—the idea that one God can answer to more than one name and assume more than one form."[3]

God often comes in the form of wind. Sometimes God enters gently into our lives, nudging us, prodding us, touching us ever so slightly to offer direction. Nicodemus once asked Jesus how one could be born again. Jesus answered, "The Spirit comes like the wind and you know not whither it comes" (John 3:8). The Spirit is like the wind coming gently into your life and unexpectedly touching and caressing your life. The Spirit gently offers direction.

Sometimes, as in Acts 2, the Spirit comes rushing into your life with a roar, pushing you through circumstances, events, chaos, tragedies, and even uprooting you as you are pointed in a new direction. The Spirit comes in a mighty way to touch your life, and you experience the power of God. Ezekiel knew something about the power of God as wind. In a vision, he stood before a valley of dry bones that symbolized Israel in its state of dejection, defeat, and hopelessness; and he cried out, "Come from the four winds, O breath, and breathe on these slain that they may live" (Ezek 37:9). Like Israel, we pray that the Spirit of God might blow the divine breath upon us and give us life once again.

Throughout the Old and New Testaments, one can read how God's Spirit fell upon selected persons. In the Old Testament, "The spirit of the LORD took possession of Gideon" (Judg 6:34); "The spirit of the LORD began to stir Samson" (Judg 13:24-25); "And the spirit of the LORD came mightily upon [Samson]" (Judg 14:6). "The

spirit of God possessed [Saul]" (1 Sam 10:10). In the New Testament, we read that the Spirit descended upon Jesus at his baptism
(Luke 3:21-22). Jesus stood up in the temple and said, "The spirit
of the Lord is upon me because he has anointed me to preach . . ."
(Luke 4:18). Paul assured the Corinthians that "God has revealed
to us through the Spirit" many things (1 Cor 2:10). He asked the
Corinthians, "Do you not know that your body is a temple of the
Holy Spirit within you?" (1 Cor 6:19). The Spirit comes into our
lives sometimes in the form of wind in a gentle way and on other
occasions in a mighty roar.

The Presence of Fire

The second symbol from Acts 2 representing God's Spirit is "the
tongues of fire" that seemed to protrude from the dove at Pentecost. The nation Israel celebrated three basic feasts—the Feast of
Tabernacles, the Passover, and Pentecost. Pentecost was the feast
day that furnished the setting for this story about the coming of the
tongues of fire. The festival came fifty days after Passover. Pentecost
was celebrated as a remembrance of the time when God gave the
commandments to the children of Israel. It was also a harvest celebration. The harvest had already been gathered and the Israelites
expressed their thanks for God's bounty. Two loaves of bread were
sacrificed to express thanksgiving to God.

The disciples were gathered in an upper room; maybe it was the
same room where they had met following the crucifixion of Christ.
It had to be a large area, however, because a host of other people were
near them. They had assembled in one accord, in unity, waiting for
the promised Spirit that Jesus said would come to anoint them. There
in that place, they felt and sensed the power and presence of God.

Luke didn't say the Spirit *was* fire but said it *looked* like fire. This
symbolism about the presence of God seems overwhelming in its
impact. The symbol of God as fire is an ancient one for Israel. God
appeared to Moses in a burning bush (Exod 3). Elijah saw the fire
of God's presence come down from heaven and consume his sacrifice when he was in competition with the gods of Baal (1 Kgs 18).
Elijah was carried off by death in a chariot of fire (2 Kgs 2:11). God

THE SPIRIT AT WORK IN THE WORLD

is depicted as a consuming fire (Lam 2:3; see Heb 12:29). In the temple, Isaiah had an experience with God and was so overcome by his encounter that he envisioned an angel touching his lips with a hot coal to purge him from his sins (Isa 6). Fire, in the Scriptures, is a sign of the vital presence of God among the people. Whenever we enter God's presence, we are made aware of our own sinfulness. Fire is often a symbol of the presence of God.

The Purifying, Transforming Presence

The tongues of fire also symbolize the purifying nature of God's presence. Just as fire can remove all the dross from the metal that is cast in its heat, so our lives are purified by the redeeming grace of the fire of God's presence. The blood of Christ cleanses us. It is like fire in its purifying, cleansing power.

On the day of Pentecost, the tongues of fire came as a purifying, transforming force. The disciples were gathered together, waiting to be filled by God. They had an empty feeling before the resurrection. Christ had been crucified. Now that he was dead, they thought everything was over. Suddenly the risen Christ appeared to them and gave them the promise of new life. He instructed them to wait until the Spirit of God came upon them. They waited to be filled by the Spirit of God. Now they would learn more of the Spirit's way. They would open themselves again to a growing experience with God. This coming of the Spirit was not the final expression of all that they would receive from God. They had to remain open to the Spirit's continuous presence so that God might fill them again and again.

As a young minister, I made a vow that I would always be open to God's Spirit. I promised to follow God down whatever avenue of new insight God took me, whatever new opportunities for service lay ahead of me, and what further thought God might provoke. No matter where it led me in my thinking, I promised I would be open so I might grow in my awareness of God and in my faith. One of the sad things about some Christians I know is that they have limited God as though they could capture God in a box. They think they have already learned all they can ever learn of God. For them, there are no surprises, no new opportunities, no fresh insights about God.

They hug the shores of familiarity, cling to their security blankets of traditionalism and orthodoxy, fearful that God will come into their minds and give new insights, new thoughts, new wine, or new ways.

God's Spirit can never be trapped or limited by our traditions, customary ways, or thoughts. God is always pushing against us to flood our perspective with opportunities to find new ways to serve and minister. No walls can contain God. No floors are too thick for God's Spirit to penetrate. God's Spirit breaks through all forms and traditions to give us newness in life. God touched the disciples, and they were transformed. They became people who were excited about sharing the good news with others; they were eager to tell others about what Christ had done. Their enthusiasm was evident, and others could sense the new power within them.

A university professor heard a man speak one time with great enthusiasm about his religion. After hearing this young man speak, the professor said, "I wish I could get the feel of a faith like that." Don't you wish you could too? Maybe there was a time when God's Spirit came into your life, and you were warmed by God's presence. But some of you, with the passing of time, have had the coal of that experience grow cool and almost lifeless. Let God's Spirit breathe upon you the purifying, transforming fire of divine presence. Let God's Spirit fan that coal back to life again. As the fire of God's experience burns within you, you will know God's transforming grace. Like the disciples, behind death you will experience life; behind the temporary you will find the eternal; instead of the end you will find a new beginning.

The Communicating Spirit

The tongues of fire also symbolize that God was communicating with men and women. What the crowd heard that day was not the ecstatic speech found in 1 Corinthians where the Christians spoke in some unknown tongue. Oh, no! They all understood in their own languages. We cannot explain the "how" of this story, but the people clearly understood. Part of what Luke may be trying to tell us in this story in Acts 2 points to the coming universalism of the gospel that was already present at Pentecost. The ability of all the listeners to understand the message was a sign that the good news was for all people of all races and nations. The universality of the gospel was realized at Pentecost. The Spirit breaks all barriers down and reaches out to people everywhere with the good news of Christ.

In the sanctuary at St. Matthews Baptist Church in Louisville, Kentucky, there is a spectacular stained-glass window of the Spirit. An image of the world is in the center of this window. Flames seem to be leaping around the world, symbolizing God's communication of the divine Spirit to all people everywhere. God continues to reach out toward all with good news. It is a universal word. God is concerned for all. "For God so loved the world that he gave his only begotten son" (John 3:16).

The image of St. Matthews Church is in the center part of the window, which focuses on God's particular concern about that particular church. One can see an image of the old church on fire and the new church as it emerges from the burned building. God's Spirit is depicted at work bringing new out of old, good out of bad, life out of destruction. God seemed to touch the people in that particular church in that particular time. God's fiery presence had inspired a vision of a new church, and the new has arisen. We now open our spirits to feel God's touch again.

Praise and Proclamation

The tongues of fire in Acts 2 also depict the praise and proclamation that was produced by their impact. Don't get distracted by the tongues and miss what they symbolize. The tongues were used to praise God and proclaim God's mighty works. The emphasis is not on the tongues but on praise and proclamation. Where there is praise, there is power. When pride is central in your life, you cannot really praise God. The disciples in this story praised God for God's mighty works that they had seen in Christ. Immediately they were misunderstood. "These guys are drunk," some said. "No, no," Peter answered. "It's early in the morning. That is not so." Sometimes people may misunderstand you when you get excited about sharing the gospel of Christ with others.

Halford Luccock, a minister and professor for many years at Yale Divinity School, told about an experience he had once with a policeman in New York City who read the DD printed after his name and asked him what it meant. Dr. Luccock told him it stood for "doctor of divinity." "Do you know," the policeman responded, "that 'DD' is the most common charge written on the police blotter? It means 'Drunk and Disorderly.'" Dr. Luccock assured him that was only a coincidence and that there was no connection of that meaning with him. As he was driving home later, he got to thinking about it and recalled that the early Christians had been accused of being drunk at Pentecost.

Instead of fervor and enthusiasm for Christ, many today are so respectable and stale that they will never be mistaken for being drunk and disorderly. Many Christians in mainline Protestant churches have lost their sense of enthusiasm, joy, and radiance. Our religion is routine and pale. Our faith was meant to be shared, not hoarded. We can speak a word for our faith with gentleness and without self-righteousness. We can use good common sense and act toward others in a way that is loving and kind. With humor and warm friendship, and without arrogance, we can share the good news. Hopefully, individuals with whom we talk can see the inner joy we have experienced in Christ and note our desire to praise God for the grace we have known. The tongues of fire are tremendous symbols for the presence of God in the lives of God's people. When we feel this presence, we will want to share it.

Those Who Serve Christ

One of the central features in the stained-glass window at St. Matthews is the line of individuals who form a series of patterns of different walks of people across the center of the window. Christ is in the center of this image. On his left there is a figure who appears to be the Apostle Paul writing letters to the early churches. Next there is a couple accompanied by a young child as they are going to work. A chef raises a dish he has prepared. He is followed by two teachers and a laborer working with a jackhammer. This side ends with missionaries sharing the word of Christ.

On the right side of Christ is a figure of a minister preaching the gospel. Beside him a young man is playing a guitar. Next is a family with a mother and father and three children. Following them is a scene that depicts someone visiting in a nursing home, hospital, or home. This scene may also include a doctor or doctors or a friend. They are accompanied by a farmer. The next figures are either scientists, medical doctors, or pharmacists, and they are followed by a fire fighter. On this end of the panel, there is an image of another missionary who is sharing the word of Christ. These various people in the window remind us of Paul's words to the Corinthians about the varieties of spiritual gifts and the many ways people can share one's spiritual gifts in ministry for Christ (1 Cor 12:1-13).

Christ at the Center

What are we to make of the symbolism in this stained-glass window? Remember that Christ is at the center. The emphasis is clear. The Spirit of God is seeking to lead men and women to commit their lives to Christ as Lord. Jesus Christ has brought in the dawn of a new day, and in him there is abundant life and redemption. The various individuals on the panel also indicate that God reaches out to speak to people in all walks of life. Christ breaks down all barriers of race and sex. God's redeeming presence reaches out to all.

Unfortunately, some of us often feel like the boy who wrote a letter that Bill Adler shares in his book *Dear Pastor*: "Dear Pastor, I know God loves everybody, but He never met my sister. Yours sincerely, Arnold."[4] I need to tell you, Arnold, that God loves little sisters and big brothers, Black and brown and white people, rich and famous people from all across life. God loves us all, and God's Spirit continuously reaches out to touch us with divine love.

The Priesthood of Believers

Notice also that God's Spirit is depicted in this window as working through all kinds of people, not just professional ministers. Paul reminded the Corinthians that the ministry of the Spirit is performed through a variety of ways and with numerous gifts (1 Cor 12:1-13).

God's ministry is not confined merely to what happens in a church building. God works through many instruments to accomplish the divine work. The laity is the ministry of the church in the world. God is at work in the bakery, with the fire fighter, at school, in the doctor's office, in the secretary's office, with the farmer in the field, in all of life.

We gather in the church so we might prepare to go back into the world to minister. The church is not calling people to a servanthood of the laity. It is calling the laity to a ministry in the world. You and I gather in church to worship, but then we go back into the world to serve Christ there. We don't serve Christ just when we gather in church on Sunday. We gather to prepare ourselves through worship to go into the world and minister in Christ's name. God works through people in many ways to minister in the world. God employs young, old, teachers, doctors, musicians, chefs, farmers, bankers, homemakers, and countless thousands of others to people's lives. God has many voices and tongues.

When Nathan Pusey was president of Harvard University, he once told a graduating class, "The finest fruit of serious learning should be the ability to speak the word 'God' without reserve or embarrassment." You as a Christian, touched by the Spirit of God, should be able to go into the world in your vocation and unashamedly live out the Christian life. Our vocation is a means to serve and glorify God.

The Fellowship of the Church

If you look carefully at this Spirit window in St. Matthews Church, you will notice that the tongues of fire seem to fall upon everyone. The tongues are even reflected in the water on the window as the presence of God penetrates all of life. The church will continue if each generation shares the gospel with the next generation. We pass on what we have experienced. We must share with others our own experience with God. Fire cannot burn well with just one log; it takes at least two. The church grows by fellowship. Our faith is kindled by the faith of others. What I have experienced, I now pass on to another. Fire manifests itself in the form of flames. It comes into the cold and brings warmth; it enters darkness and brings light; it touches the defiled and brings purity. God has broken into our lives, and God has touched you and me. God's fiery presence has made us different. Now we are challenged to reach out and touch others—not to contain God's Spirit but to pass it on. We reach out and touch one another.

When I was in England a number of years ago, I visited the Coventry Cathedral. This cathedral was destroyed by fire during the Second World War and was later rebuilt. A book was written about this church titled *Fire in Coventry*, but it wasn't about the bombing and the physical burning of the church. It was about what happened to the church after it was rebuilt, when a different kind of fire broke out within it. A sense of the vitality of God's Spirit came into that congregation and renewed it. This renewal came about because laypeople within the church were set aglow by the Spirit, power, and presence of God.

St. Matthews Baptist Church's building is depicted in its stained-glass window as rising up out of destruction to begin a new life. The building, however, will never be the church. If God's people are really to be what God would have us be, you and I will have to experience the kindling flame of God's renewal. When our lives have been set aglow by contact with the fire of God's Spirit, we, in turn, will set others on fire. The church is everywhere.

When I visited a woman in the hospital recently, I embraced her as I was leaving, and she said, "Thank you for doing that. Nobody ever hugs me anymore." There are a lot of people who are waiting for somebody to reach out and embrace them, to share love, to share a touch, to share hope, or to share opportunities.

I pray that God's Spirit may come into our lives. If you do not know God, may God ignite you with the divine presence. If you have known God in your life and have grown cold, may God come into your life anew with the warmth of the divine presence and fan your faith into a glowing fire for service. For those who have gotten into frozen apathy and indifference, may God's warm presence and radiance thaw you and bring you into newness of life. May the radiance of God's love and presence give you direction and meaning in your life. I pray that every church might truly be a church that is on fire with God's presence. May we exhibit a burning glow that says to all, "God is here. God is near, and I have seen God. I have seen God here in this place."

Chapter 10

A Family of Faith
1 Corinthians 12:12-23

When I was a local pastor, from time to time people asked me, "Where is your church located?" These were people who may not have lived in our community for long. Some people would ask, "How big is your church?" "How many ministers do you have on staff?" They asked questions about what the church did or what our basic purpose was.

The Vision Committee in my church in North Carolina wrestled for some time with identifying our church's basic distinctive. I challenged them to try to put this distinctive in one sentence so that we could see it and state it clearly. And they did. We printed that sentence in our bulletin: "First Baptist Church is a family of faith seeking to know Christ, worshiping together, and sharing His love through missions and ministry." Think with me about what that statement means.

The Meaning of Family

Let's look first at the meaning of "a family of faith." We all understand something about what a family is. A healthy family is a group of people who love, accept, and care for one another. We all want to feel that the church can be a place where we are loved, accepted, and cared for.

A small boy once said, "A family is someone who sticks with you when everybody else walks away." We need that kind of family at church. When we acknowledge our own weaknesses and sinfulness, we need to have the assurance that the family of faith is with us to nurture us, to bear us up, to minister to our needs, and to show genuine love and support.

The Church as a Body

Paul used an interesting image of the church. Some call it a metaphor, and others call it a parable. He wrote that the church is a body and important. Every single part has value, whether it is an eye, an ear, an arm, or a leg. Every part of the body is essential. As applied to the church, all of the body is a part of the totality. Everyone is a part of Christ.

In drawing from Paul's image, I have often wondered, if the church is the body of Christ, what do we say about those who are inactive and non-resident members? What happens to the body of Christ if a person who is an arm or a leg or an eye is inactive or never present? We know this harms the body of the church. Think what it means to speak of an arm or a leg as missing. As a church, we don't seem to be very concerned. If we lost something precious at home, or lost it anyplace, think how many endless hours we would spend looking for it, groping for it, to bring it back and make it a part of our possessions once more. Sometimes we seem unconcerned about those who have drifted away from the church. And the inactive seem unconcerned that they are not a vital part of the body of Christ.

A Challenge to Be Active

Allen Neely, a Baptist who taught at Princeton Divinity School, said that he was invited once to speak to a Mennonite church in Goshen, Indiana. They wanted him to come for what they called "renewal services." These renewal services last for one month, and during this month the members are given an opportunity to come anytime, day or night, and sign the church book if they want to continue to be a member. They have to sign the book every three years to indicate anew their commitment to the church.

I wonder how this would affect the membership in our churches. Would it drastically reduce our membership? But maybe it would result in a more realistic figure of what the church membership genuinely is. Those who have been separated from the family need to be brought back into the fellowship.

When we lived in Louisville, I remember reading about a man whose hand was cut off by a piece of farm machinery. He was rushed to Jewish Hospital in Louisville, with his severed hand packed in ice. The surgeons worked for about ten hours to reattach his hand, and they were able to save it. The church needs to reach out to the lost eyes, lost ears, lost legs and arms and bring them back to make them a part of the body of Christ. We are a family. We should love one another and be concerned about those who are severed from the family.

Seeking to Know Christ

We are a family of faith, and that leads us to the second part of our church's mission statement. As a family of faith, we are "seeking to know Christ." We attest that we strive for a regenerate church membership. Our members are people who have committed their lives to Jesus Christ as Lord and been baptized. We do not declare a secondhand faith; we claim that we have a personal experience with Christ. Having committed our lives to Christ, we are seeking to know Christ. This should be our basic thrust through Sunday school, worship, and everything else we do. Our goal is to understand Christ more fully and to be more like him. We want to be more like him in how we live and in our understanding of what is meaningful in life.

As Christians, we believe that Jesus Christ has revealed to us the nature of God—redemptive, suffering love. We look to Jesus Christ as the One who through his life and teachings revealed to us God's love and grace. Through his death on the cross and his resurrection, we see the redemptive love of God drawing humanity back to God's self. We look to Christ as our example in how to serve God and as the model for the more effective life.

When I was a young pastor in Harrisonburg, Virginia, an older retired minister shared something unforgettable with me on Sunday as he walked through my door. He shook hands with me that day and made some positive comments. Then he said, "Bill, let me encourage you always to preach about Jesus. Always share the words about Jesus with your congregation." I have never forgotten those words. In all of our preaching and teaching, we seek to share the message of the good news of what God has done through Christ and what we have seen revealed about God through Christ. In our Sunday school, our worship, and our other groups, we seek to enable people to get closer to God through their awareness of what God has done through Jesus Christ.

William Willimon, who was the chaplain at Duke University, said that one day when he was a pastor, his six-year-old son said, "Daddy, I don't want to go to Sunday school. We never do anything different there. It is always the same old thing. Jesus! Jesus! Jesus!"

Well, that's what the church is. It is about the same old thing. Jesus! Jesus! Jesus! Church is about Jesus and what he tells us about God. It is about how we can grow in our awareness of God and how we can love and serve God more effectively. We are "seeking to know Christ." As Paul says, "We are to live our lives in Christ."

The Summons to Continuous Growth

Seeking to know Christ is not a onetime, momentary experience. The tragedy and heresy of the Baptist denomination is that we have gotten some people to think that because they make a onetime commitment, their relationship to God is complete and everything is all right forever in that relationship. I have never forgotten the sermon of a Baptist preacher who declared, "You must be born again, and again, and again, and again." What was he saying? He was echoing the words of the Apostle Paul. "I was saved. I am being saved. And I will be saved." No one has ever arrived spiritually. There are always areas in our lives that need converting. There are always places in our lives that need to be redeemed. There are always prejudices and dark corners that need to be overcome and swept clean and transformed. We need to be reborn again and again in our relationship to God. The whole concept of the new birth is about a spiritual beginning. It requires growth.

"Seeking to know Christ" is being aware that we must keep growing, keep developing, and keep opening ourselves to the power and grace of God. "Unless religion leads us on a path to both depth and honesty, so much religion is actually quite dangerous to the soul and to society," Richard Rohr writes. "In fact," he continues, "'fast-food religion' and the so-called prosperity gospel are some of the very ways to actually avoid God—while talking about religion almost nonstop."[1] Talking about our faith on a superficial level may indicate our lack of depth in spiritual awareness. We must open ourselves to what draws us beyond our self-interest and personal security to what pulls us to higher values and ministries. Jesus is drawing us toward spiritual wholeness, which is a lifetime journey. Notice how many of Jesus's parables focus on growth, like seed or corn growing, wheat and weeds growing together, yeast rising, and more. As Christians, growth is an essential part of our spiritual nature.

The Central Act of Worship

The First Baptist Church is a family of faith seeking to know Christ, "worshiping together." The central act of the church is worship. The central focus of the church is worship together. If you only attend Sunday school, youth groups, or mission groups and do not gather and worship together at church, you are severing yourself from the corporate act of the church and the most essential event. Worship is as essential as food is for the human body, as light is for the eye to see, as sound is for the ear to hear, as air is for the body to breathe. Not worshiping means cutting oneself off from God and the possibility of growth and development. Worship is essential.

I worship out of my own awareness of my vulnerability. The vulnerability of human life flashes before the minds of millions across the world whenever a tragedy hits. We are aware that every single person is vulnerable. No person can meet all of their own needs. We open ourselves in worship to sense the grace of God. We should worship out of a sense of thanksgiving to open ourselves to commune with God and express gratitude to God for the bountiful blessings we have received in life. A grateful heart wants to worship.

I worship out of the awesome sense of the mystery of God and the mystery of life. Worship to me is like standing under a waterfall with a cup that I am trying to fill. There is no way I can keep my cup level because the waterfall keeps filling the cup to overflowing again and again. Worship is lifting up our spiritual cups so God will fill them with God's presence and our lives might be refreshed, transformed, renewed, and strengthened.

The church has a hard time doing worship today because of what a lot of folks want. In the *Kudzu* comic strip, a woman goes to her preacher and complains to him, "What—no tanning salon? No juice bars! No food courts! No fitness centers! No jacuzzi! No sauna! No skating rink! And you call yourself a house of worship?" What do people want the church to be? Everything! Whatever they desire, that's what they expect the church to be. But the church is *not* everything. It focuses on the One True Thing so that we can worship and expose ourselves to the power and grace of God. We worship together.

I am thankful for all the other groups we have in our church. They are important. Every small group provides fellowship and community, but Sunday school and Bible studies are not worship. Our mission groups are not worship. Our youth groups are not worship. We need to learn to come together as a congregation, young and old. We need to come together as people of every age who are aware that we learn from each other—that youth learn from the old and the old learn from the youth. We share something with each other as we gather together in church.

One of the tragedies in seeking to isolate the church by age, sex, or some other means is that we limit our possibility of learning from those who may be different from us. Whether we are single or couples or youth or children or adults, genuine worship is not done in some specialized way. When it is, that's only the way that particular group thinks worship should always be like.

When I was a younger pastor, I was offered the opportunity to serve as the first chaplain for the University of Richmond. That was exciting for me in many ways. I had pastored a university church and a college church and enjoyed working with college students and preaching to them. My family was willing to move, and the job offered a real challenge. But I was concerned that I had to preach each Sunday in chapel. I knew it would be exciting to lead these services, but I ultimately decided not to go. My reason? Because those services would offer students a format of worship that they could never have again; they would never again find a worship service that focused solely on their age group or was designed for their specific needs. I would be contributing to a problem for them later in life. To offer them something unique might be wonderful on that college campus, but when they graduated they would never find a church like that. Consequently, some of them would stop going to worship. I didn't want to be a party to that because I feel so strongly about the importance of the local church.

Whatever we do for our young people, children, singles, couples, or anybody else, we need to help all of them realize that we must come together to worship as the body of Christ. I hope every church will continue to work hard at that goal.

The Importance of Missions

We are a family of faith seeking to know Christ, worshiping together and "sharing the love of God through missions and ministry." At some point, someone shared the love of Christ with me and with you. You and I would not know about Christ or his church if someone had not shared that love with us. Parents, a Sunday school teacher, a minister, a friend, or someone else shared the good news of Christ with you. A part of your responsibility and mine is to share the love of Christ with others. That is the challenge! That is the commission we have from Christ—to go into all the world and share the good news with all people so that they can come into a vital relationship with Christ as Lord. We do that through missions.

Mission takes many shapes and forms. A part of the mission of the churches I have served as pastor is giving our financial resources. In our church budgets, through our foreign, home, state, and other kinds of offerings, we give thousands of dollars to many areas of mission work. For example, in one of my churches we supported the mission work of the Cooperative Baptist Fellowship. We gave to our Baptist state and association work. We gave to support the BSU at Pembroke. We supported the Baptist Joint Committee, Wake Forest Divinity School, Richmond Theological Seminary, Gardner-Webb Divinity School, and the International Seminary at Prague. We supported the Hispanic Mission, the Baptist House of Divinity at Duke, the Campbell Divinity School, and a host of others through our gifts. All of this is vital and important. We want to give because through our financial gifts, we help fund mission work where you and I personally cannot go.

Hands-on Ministry

We were also involved in hands on ministry in the churches I served. We were challenged to do ministry in our own community and to work with those in our own backyard who had tremendous needs. We supported work at the Pastoral Care Center, a ministry in our community that our church shared in through the work of Dr. John Mackey. There was mission work at the Boys and Girls Club, where they needed tutors and others to help in various activities. We also engaged in ministries in our local nursing homes and other local mission causes. In these types of hands-on ministries, we were involved in a personal way to show the love of Christ. Robin W. Lovin, a professor at Loyola University Chicago, reminds us that "Food services, homeless ministries, children's programs, and services for the elderly [which I interpret as mission projects] all offer proven models that transform the lives of participants, both those who are served and those who provide the services."[2] Those of us who reach out in love to others are changed by our ministry as much as those who are recipients of our services.

I got up early about twenty-five ago to watch the funeral service for Princess Diana, who had been killed in an automobile accident. One of the interesting things to me in the telecast was the comments made about her charity work with the underprivileged, those who suffered with AIDS and HIV, lepers, and the homeless and outcast. Diana had been a member of the royal family, yet she chose to support some important charity causes.

Not even a week later in the same year, 1997, Mother Teresa, who reached out to the poorest of the poor in Calcutta, India, died at the age of eighty-seven. An article described how she first started her work. She saw a woman who was dying on the street. Maggots were already in the woman's body, and rats were eating her flesh. Mother

Teresa stayed with her until she died. She begged the city officials for a home where she could take such people to care for them until they died. She got a house. Then the neighbors began to complain. They didn't want this kind of house in their neighborhood. The authorities came and investigated. They saw the plight of the tragic people whom she and other nuns were helping. The officials said to the neighbors, "When you and your mothers and others will take care of these people, then we will close the house." These nuns were caring for society's outcasts. I cannot imagine anything going on in our world today that was more Christlike. Christ has called all of us to be a part of missions and ministry.

We have to decide. Does the church focus primarily on maintenance—keeping programs going, taking care of our building, making sure our members are happy and satisfied? Or do we focus on what Christ has called us to do—to minister, to reach out and help others in the world? We have to make a decision as the church. Of course, we need to maintain our buildings, but are we going to do the kinds of ministries that Christ has called us to do to share the good news with people in the world? We are called to be a people who are concerned about others no matter what their needs might be. Is the church ready to accept that challenge?

The church ought to be the place where the family of God reaches out to those who need a hug and embraces them with the love of Christ. It ought to be a place where individuals can gather together and offer their troubled spirits to God so that God can touch their lives with peace. It ought to be a place where an individual who has a need can come and find the support of the community of faith. It ought to be a place where an individual who is burdened with sins or cares can unload these burdens before God and find forgiveness and new opportunities to begin again. It ought to be a place where a person whose family is torn apart can come and find in the family of faith a supportive group to minister to them and undergird them. I hope that the church can genuinely be the kind of family of faith that God wants us to be, where we will seek to know Christ, worship together, and share God's love through missions and ministry. God give us the strength and guidance to do that.

Chapter 11

The Greatest of These Is Love

1 Corinthians 13:1-13

In the novel *Point of No Return*, John P. Marquand wrote that one of his characters knew all of the little answers but never asked the big questions. It's that way for a lot of us. We simply never raise the larger questions about the meaning of life. For example, some people do not ask the question, "What is the greatest power in the world?" Is it political, military, or monetary? What is it? Today, we might hear all kinds of answers to that question. I believe that love is the greatest force in the world. Dean Ornish wrote that "our survival depends on the healing power of love, intimacy, and relationships."[1] Karl Menninger has said that "our mental health depends on our capacity to love."[2] Rollo May has written, "To be capable of giving and receiving mature love is as sound a criterion as we have for the fulfilled personality."[3] I believe that we really cannot be complete, full people without love.

Love, however, seems like such a fragile word. To say that love is the greatest force in the world sounds absurd to some. Love sounds like a mushy, overly romantic word. Love often seems soft, mild, a pie-in-the-sky ideal, an otherworldly attitude, and is sometimes thought to depict weakness instead of strength.

The Young Church in Corinth

The Apostle Paul wrote about love (1 Cor 13:1-13) to a worldly church in Corinth. This church was located in a commercial center in southern Greece. It was filled with praying and playing, singing and swaying, gluttony and greed, lying and laughter. It was known for its immorality, envy, jealousy, emotionalism, pride, fanaticism, strife, bad theology, and other problems. It had the characteristics of a lot of contemporary churches today, but worse. It was a church torn apart by divisions.

One might ask, "Why would Paul want to send a hymn about love to this particular church?" Some scholars stated that this hymn of love was from the hand of somebody else, and Paul simply inserted it at this particular point in his letter to the Corinthians. If you read the argument of the hymn carefully, however, you will notice that Paul is addressing the very issue that he has written about up to this point. He has been discussing the divisiveness in the church and the need to recognize the diversity of gifts within the church. There is no question in my mind that this is Paul's writing.

The Love Hymn

The hymn in 1 Corinthians is not a poem in meter; it is written in prose. This prose seems to sing and dance across the page into the reader's eye or into the hearer's ear and into one's heart and life. It is filled with vitality and strikingly original images. It almost seems that an angel has touched Paul's pen.

When we examine 1 Corinthians 13, we may be cautious about touching what seems to be such a fragile piece of writing. Some people approach it like a crystal bowl of rare beauty with exquisite cut and design. They fear that if they touch it, it might shatter. But do not fear. This hymn of love has survived examining, touching, telling, and preaching for centuries. It is a sound work and will stand the strain of careful examination.

The Greatest Gift in the Church

To begin with, notes that Paul is not saying that love in general is the greatest thing in the world. He is not speaking about love in the world. He writes that love is the *greatest gift in the church*. He is describing the kind of love that Christians should have in their lives. The love depicted in this chapter is not love that just anybody can have. It is Christian love. It is the love a genuine disciple of Christ has in their life. "Love," according to J. Paul Sampley, is the absolutely indispensable feature of the believing life.[4]

Love Contrasted with Other Gifts

The Gift of Speech

Paul begins by contrasting love with other gifts (vv. 1-3). He contrasts love first with the *gift of speech*. There were many people in that day who thought the most important way to speak to God was by using ecstatic utterances, like an unknown tongue. This ecstatic speech was popular in pagan worship. Sometimes pagan rites, like the worship of Dionysus, would have a religious procession and sound cymbals or ring bells to call people to worship. Paul said this kind of speaking was just a noisy gong if the speaker did not have love.

Spiritual Instruction

Next Paul contrasts love with prophecy-inspired preaching, a great faith, and the knowledge of all the mysteries of life. This is a reference to three kinds of *spiritual instruction*. The church had been torn apart by those loyal to the preaching of Peter and Apollos and Paul. Paul was reminding the Corinthians, "You can be the greatest preacher in the world, but if you really don't love people, it doesn't make any difference."

We have all known preachers who were powerful speakers, but they lacked character because they had no love. You have seen preachers, as I have, who were gifted speakers, but they preached hate. They communicated "I hate you" and "God hates you." George Adams Smith once asked a Greek churchman why he thought God had made so many Moslems. This man's church had suffered greatly under Islam. "God made Moslems simply to furnish fire for hell," the churchman said. Such a harsh and unloving statement makes us recoil today. There are some preachers who preach brilliantly, but their preaching is filled with anger and hatred. Without love, their preaching is futile. Just because a person preaches in the name of

Christ does not make that preaching authentic. To say "Lord, Lord" is not enough. To some, Jesus will say, "I never knew you."

Philanthropy and Self-sacrifice

Paul also contrasted love with *philanthropy and self-sacrifice*. This is charity at its highest. A person may give everything they have for charity or even be consumed in a ball of fire in the name of God, but if they don't have love, it is worthless. Why? The motive is wrong. They do what they do to call attention to themselves. A person may give and be ostentatious. It may be for prestige or self-glory.

Paul may have been referring to giving one's body to be burned to a monument in Corinth that was erected by a man from India, who set himself on fire. He left an inscription to be put on the monument stating that he had given himself immortality by this act. The Greeks had a saying: "He roasted himself to boast." That doesn't gain a person anything with God.

Our motive is central in our charity and sacrifice. We can do the right thing for the wrong reason. If there is no love, no matter how large the gift or apparent sacrifice, it is worthless in God's sight. Jesus told about the scribes and Pharisees, who would have trumpets sound in the streets before they would pray in the temple in order to call the people to come and listen to them pray. Jesus said, "They have their reward." What was their reward? They wanted people to hear them pray, and people heard them. But they could forget about God hearing that prayer. Their reward was to be seen and heard by other people.

The Characteristics of Love

In verses 4-7, Paul gives us the *characteristics of love*. Henry Drummond, in his address on this hymn, says that this section is like a crystal prism through which light shines and casts its rays on the other side.[5] All of these different-colored beams of light give us some characteristics of what love is like. Paul enumerates some of the virtues of the Christian faith. Here we see love in action.

Love Is Patient

Paul begins by saying that love is *patient*. It means we learn how to wait. We don't expect everything good to happen in a moment. We plant a seed, and then we step back and wait. If there is anything that is characteristic of God, it is patience. God is long-suffering. Love learns to endure strain as it waits.

Love Is Kind

Love is *kind*. It is gentle and magnanimous. It does not want to do anything to hurt others but desires what is best for them.

Love Is Not Jealous

Love is *not jealous*. It doesn't look at another person's success and say, "Oh, how did she get that?" "How could that happen to him?" Love is not jealous because its ultimate values are not material ends but spiritual goals. It is generous in praise to others who succeed.

Love Does Not Call Attention to Its Self

Love does not brag; it is *not arrogant*. A loving Christian is humble and doesn't spend all the time seeking attention and saying, "Look at how great I am in God's kingdom." When I was pastor of St. Matthews Baptist Church in Louisville, a number of professors from the Southern Baptist Theological Seminary were members of our church. On one Sunday morning, Dr. Charles Scalise, who was then professor of theology and church history at SBTS, was giving a stewardship testimony. In his remarks he stated that his small son was once asked what his father did for a living. His son's response was, "He teaches the children's choir at church." Isn't that an interesting characteristic of a professor of theology? But it indicates something about Dr. Scalise's humble, quiet work in his local church.

In our church in Louisville, a number of other professors of theology and students worked in their church in many roles of service. They gave their lives to God by serving on ordinary church committees and taking responsibilities without seeking to call attention to themselves. Love is not arrogant and boastful. Real love is not ashamed to do humble, even degrading tasks for our Lord.

Love Does Not Strut and Is Not Selfish

Love does *not act unbecomingly*. It is not puffed up. It doesn't strut around. Love does not always seek its own end. It is not selfish. It is gracious and kind toward others.

I read about a man in Massachusetts a number of years ago who drowned. He was walking along the pier, tripped over a rope that had secured a boat to the shore, and fell into the water. He immediately came to the surface and, being unable to swim, screamed for help. His friends heard him, but they were too far away to get to him.

There was a man in a deck chair sunbathing near where the drowning man fell in. The sunbather was a good swimmer. Nevertheless, he just lay there and watched the man drown and did not do a thing. The family was so upset by the man's lack of response that they sued him. But the court ruled that there was nothing the law could do. There is no law that says a person has to help somebody who is drowning.

But there is a law, I believe. It is the law of love and compassion. It is the law of humanity. When we have Christian love, we do not seek what we can get out of life and how our comforts can be met. We seek to help.

Love Is Not Easily Irritated

This Christian love is also *not easily provoked*. It doesn't fly into a rage every time something doesn't go its own way. Love is not irritated to the point it blows its stack all the time, because the person is out of control. It learns not to be easily irritated and to be the master of moods.

Love Does Not Keep Score

This love also does not take into account a wrong that is suffered. It does not keep score of the times a person has done something wrong to hurt someone. This figure is taken from the work of an accountant. Love does not keep a ledger or a notebook and make a list of the wrongs of others.

One day, a mother was punishing her young son who had been naughty at home, and she put him in the closet. I do not agree with this form of discipline, but it is what she did. When she put her son in the closet, he was screaming and crying. Finally, he calmed down. The mother opened the door and asked, "Jimmy, what are you doing?" "I have spit on your shoes," he said. "I have spit on your dresses. I have spit on your coat. I have spit on your hats. I am sitting here now waiting to get some more spit so I can spit again!"

Too many people in life are just like that, aren't they? Their whole lives are filled with waiting to see if they can spit back at you for something you have done to them. But Paul says love does not keep account of the wrongs that have been suffered.

Love Does Not Gloat

Love also does not rejoice in the sins of others. Love does not gloat over other people's troubles. It doesn't read the paper and say, "Boy, did you see what happened to Jack? It's about time he got what's coming to him." Real love does not rejoice in wrong but realizes the pain and disgrace that come in these circumstances. Love rejoices in the truth because truth is the nature of God.

Love Is Vicarious

Love bears all things. It shoulders the burdens of others. Real love is vicarious. It is schooled in patience. It waits for God to bring good out of the worst circumstances. Christian love hurts with others, feels their pain, senses their need, aches with their remorse and guilt, and longs with them for assurance, hope, encouragement, and grace. It puts a shoulder under the loads of others and seeks to help them.

Love Believes All Things

Love also believes all things. It is trusting. Paul is referring here mainly to weaker Christians. He encouraged stronger Christians in Corinth who had witnessed some unbelievable sins and weaknesses in others to continue to believe in them. They had been touched by Christ. They were still immature, but Paul urged them to try to see the good, the possibilities, and the hopes that those weaker Christians might have.

Love Hopes All Things

This love also hopes during all things. For the Christian, hope is like bright stars in the darkest of skies. Hope provides steps that lead over the valley of destruction or discouragement. Hope shines like the sun that rises at the dawn of a new day to light the path of new opportunities and ideas.

Love Is Enduring

Love endures all things. Christian love is willing to serve in a place that is hard and difficult, without recognition or prestige. It will serve faithfully even when there is misunderstanding or ridicule because this love models itself after Christ. It enables a person to serve with grace and poise in the worst situations.

A Reversal of Love

If you want to know what the Corinthian church was like, reverse these characteristics of love. That is what the church was like. That is the reason Paul wrote this letter to them. The church was jealous, full of strife, keeping accounts of wrongs, arrogant, rude, unkind, impatient, angry, and the reverse of all the other things Paul mentions here. If you want to have insight into the difficulty of fulfilling this particular hymn, insert your name in place of "love" and see how you fit. How would it read to say, "Joe Smith or Jane Jones is patient and kind, not angry . . ."? Remember that this love should be characteristic of the Christian. Love is the true measure of a Christian, not a doctrine or rites.

The Permanence of Love

First Corinthians 13 concludes with Paul speaking of the permanence of love: "Love never fails." Love does not fail because love endures (vv. 8-13). Love seems in some ways as fragile and brief as the flight and life of a butterfly. It appears weak and soft.

But no. The word "fails" comes from a word in Greek that means "does not disappear." We have given this word the opposite of its original meaning. Love is unconquerable. The religious authorities thought they had finished Jesus when they crucified him on a cross. But no! There was the resurrection! The love of Christ could not be stopped by death. It was victorious over the grave. The love of Christ continues to cast its glow into the world.

E. Stanley Jones, the famous missionary, told about a visit he made one night to an ancient Syrian Christian church in Travancore, India. Hanging from the ceiling at the center of the church was a huge old brass candelabrum with about a hundred arms, each holding a little cup filled with oil and a wick. At the close of the evening worship service, the young people came up and took one of the cups to guide them in the darkness.[6] That is what the Christian love of Christ does for us. It gives us light amid the darkness in our world. We carry his love to guide us. Love is a light that continues to brighten our pathway. It is imperishable.

Love Contrasted Again

Paul closes his argument by saying that prophecies—inspired preaching, tongues, and knowledge—will pass away. He contrasts love with these three again and notes that our knowledge and languages will one day be seen as inadequate. Some ancient languages have already disappeared in our world. Even our greatest knowledge is pale in comparison to love. These things will vanish. Why? They belong to the immature, physical world.

Our knowledge in this world is imperfect. Our knowledge of God and everything else we know is like a small child's knowledge. It is immature and partial. Our knowledge of God is like the reflection we see in a polished mirror. Paul isn't talking about a glass mirror. They didn't have those in his time. They had polished metal mirrors that gave an imperfect and distorted reflection. "This is what our knowledge of God is really like," Paul says. In the spiritual realm, we will have a more perfect knowledge.

Love Is Permanent

Why is love permanent? This love is the supreme gift because it is derived from the nature of God. God is love. God is both the source of our love and the object of our love. We love because God first loved us. Human love is drawn from the well of the deep waters of God's abiding grace, and this water is shared with other human beings for a drink from the cup of God's love.

Love Does Not Fail

Why does love never fail? Paul says it is the crown of all the virtues. "Now abides faith, hope, and love, these three." Paul uses an interesting construction in Greek. Faith, hope, and love take a singular verb. This is not a slip of the pen for Paul. I think it is deliberately done. He uses these three nouns together as though they were one emphasis. Faith, hope, and love, all three, abide beyond this earthly realm.

Hope Is the Minister of Strength

Hope abides because it is "the minister of strength." We cling to "the hope of glory" and follow "the God of hope." Hope is what gives us an eternal, continuous leap, longing and drive to move on. Hope assures us that there is still more yet to be. "Christian love is made possible by hope," Andrew Lester states. "Love is excited about the here and now, but this excitement is attached to anticipation about the tomorrows."[7]

Faith Is the Eye of the Soul

Faith abides—continues—because faith is "the eye of the soul"; it is our spiritual insight. Faith gives us the willingness to step into the unknown sea before us with confidence that God will provide a path. Faith gives us this assurance as we step into the door of death. We have faith that God's embracing arms will meet us there.

Love Is the Root of Faith and Hope

Love abides and is superior because love is the root of both faith and hope. Paul says, "Love believes all things; love hopes all things." Love then gives birth to and nurtures both hope and faith. Christian love is rooted in God's being.

When you and I are attached to God, we are radically different. Love draws its breath from the God who first loves. Love is the quality of our being a child of God by faith and hope.

Cultivate the Spiritual Gift of Love

Cultivate these spiritual gifts. But remember that the greatest gift of all is love. I can't speak for you, but I know that I am a long way from living this kind of life of love. I would suggest that each of us read 1 Corinthians 13 daily for several months. Let our being be saturated by these words. Pray over them, meditate on them, and seek to cultivate in your life the love that Paul writes about here. This Christian virtue, if practiced, could radically transform our individual lives, our churches, our nation, and the whole world. If this love really became a reality, think how different the church and world would be.

Helen Battle wrote a book titled *Every Wall Shall Fall.*[8] In it, she tells about her experience of trying to rescue an American who was trapped on the eastern side of the Berlin Wall. In her attempt to rescue her friend, she was captured and imprisoned. Another prisoner took a dislike to Helen and slandered her to the matron, who put her into solitary confinement. She knew she could not stand that existence very long, and she contemplated suicide.

One day she happened to pick up a German Bible and read Paul's chapter on love in 1 Corinthians 13. As she read it, she thought, "How radical this love is. Here is the key to a real revolution! Not the violence bred from hatred or injustice, but a great justice in this dynamic conquering love." So she decided to wait.

Two days later the warden called her in. He had read the letter she had written home. She had indicated that it was probably her last letter. He could tell that she was depressed, and he said to her, "You can't lose courage. You can't lose hope. Christianity is the way of the cross." "That from a Marxist!" she thought.

She didn't lose hope. She went back to prison and gave courage and hope to the other prisoners. Even the woman who had mistreated her said, "I am glad that I have come to prison; otherwise I never would have met you." Eventually she was released. But during imprisonment she found hope and encouragement in reading this hymn of love in Paul's Epistle to the Corinthians.

Love is the greatest gift in the Christian life. Let us cultivate this gift with all of our strength. Let us continue to draw encouragement and guidance from this passage on how to live in today's world. Read again this text in the translation by J. B. Phillips.

If I speak with the eloquence of men or women and of angels, but have not love, I become no more than blaring brass or crashing cymbal. If I have the gift of foretelling the future and hold in my mind not only all human knowledge but the very secrets of God, and if I also have that absolute faith which can move mountains, but have no love, I amount to nothing at all. If I dispose of all that I possess, yes, even if I give my own body to be burned, but have no love, I achieve precisely nothing.

This love of which I speak is slow to lose patience—it looks for a way of being constructive. It is not possessive: it is neither anxious to impress nor does it cherish inflated ideas of its own importance.

Love has good manners and does not pursue selfish advantage. It is not touchy. It does not keep account of evil or gloat over the wickedness of other people. On the contrary, it is glad with all good men and women when truth prevails.

Love knows no limit to its endurance, no end to its trust, no fading of its hope; it can outlast anything. It is, in fact, the one thing that still stand when all else has fallen.

For if there are prophecies they will be fulfilled and done with, if there are "tongues" the need for them will disappear, if there is knowledge it will be swallowed up in truth. For our knowledge is always incomplete and our prophecy is always incomplete, and when the complete comes, that is the end of the incomplete.

When I was a little child I talked and felt and thought like a little child. Now that I am a man or woman my childish speech and feeling and thought have no further significance for me.

At present we are men and women looking at puzzling reflections in a mirror. The time will come when we shall see reality whole and face to face! At present all I know is a little fraction of the truth, but the time will come when I shall know it as fully as God now knows me!

In this life we have three great lasting qualities—faith, hope, and love. But the greatest of them is love.[9]

Chapter 12

Apathy: Life as a Spectator

1 Corinthians 13

Debbie Jean was lost. At the moment, that was all that really mattered to her family. Her father had been working upstairs in his study. It was his responsibility to look after the children that afternoon. His wife had gone shopping. The young girl had come in from school, taken a nap, and then played with her four-year-old brother for a while. But now her father could not find her. Her mother arrived home and they both looked desperately for her. "Where could she be?" they wondered. They walked down the familiar path she often used. They did not find her playing in the places where she so often played. The father quickly traced her steps to her school, but the principal did not know where she was.

They spent two hours looking for her but could not find her anywhere. Just as her father was getting ready to call the police, Debbie Jean came walking around the corner of the school. She had left the house to go to the home of a friend, and they had walked to a candy store a short distance away. She hadn't thought about the time. After the thunder and lightning and tears died down, her father reflected on what had happened. He had letters to write during that time, articles to write, books to read, much work that he needed to do. But during those two hours, the only thing he thought about was his daughter. He was concerned primarily for her. That was his central concern.

Care Is a Powerful Emotion

At certain moments in our lives, care erupts as a powerful emotion. Numerous concerns take priority and are pushed forward into our minds in such a significant way that we cannot ignore them. We often acknowledge that care is a powerful emotion in our society. We say this when we take a package to the post office and ask them if they will stamp on it, "Handle with Care." Some of you have sent care packages to service members overseas. College students often talk about receiving "care packages" from home. Sometimes, as we are driving down a two-lane road, we see a sign that cautions us to "Pass with Care." We all enjoy giving or receiving "tender loving care." One of our greeting card companies has a slogan declaring that you mail their cards "when you care enough to send the very best."

But I suppose one of the most common expressions we use to illustrate our attitude toward care is what we say when somebody expresses something unkind about us: "Well, I couldn't care less." What we mean deep inside is "I wish I didn't care so much." Care is indeed a powerful emotion. Its absence leaves a void.

You may have seen the headlines several years ago in a Dayton, Ohio, newspaper that read, "Woman Drowns as Her Screams for Help Are Ignored." She drowned in a river while she was surrounded by a crowd of people who were swimming. No one responded to her cries for help, and she drowned. In 1964, in Queens, New York, Kitty Genovese was robbed and stabbed to death within sight of her neighbors. As she screamed for help, her neighbors closed their windows and turned back to their televisions and newspapers. Headlines that followed claimed "37 Who Saw Murder Didn't Call the Police."

Some Choose Not to Get Involved

Apathy is a bad policy. But unfortunately, too many people have drifted into that style of life. Would you not agree with me that for many people today, apathy or uncaring has almost become a way of life? Some of you may find that this is the attitude and approach you take toward life. "I don't want to get involved," you say. "I am going to stand on the sidelines." "If I get involved, I may be misunderstood."

"I may be misquoted." "Someone may make fun of me." "It will take time, effort, and energy." "I will stand back and let others take care of this." We see that attitude reflected again and again in our society. We had rather be spectators. We want to sit in the back of life and not up near the front. If we get involved, somebody might saw off the limb where we sit, or we might be exposed and our true feelings made apparent. Somebody might poke fun at us. So we do not get involved at all.

A high school girl wrote a letter several years ago to her minister. "I have been thinking this year about the importance of caring, of passion in life," she wrote. "I have often realized that it takes courage to care. Caring is dangerous; it leaves you open to hurt and to looking a fool; and perhaps it is because they have been hurt so often that people are afraid to care. You can't die if you are not alive, but then who would rather be a stone?"

Simon & Garfunkel have a song titled "I Am a Rock." Their words still echo in my mind.

> Don't talk of love. Well,
> I've heard the word before.
> It's sleeping in my memory;
> I won't disturb the slumber
> Of feelings that have died.
> If I never loved, I never would have cried.
> I am a rock, I am an island.

Some people who have attempted to love have felt rebuffed, and so they are not able to love anymore. They have pulled back into their shells like turtles and seek to be an island alone, untouched, unmoved, not washed over by the lives of others. "I am remote, distant, apart from others," they cry. "I remain untouched."

Apathy in Our Churches

Apathy is seen not only within our society, but unfortunately it has also moved within our churches. Not many of us want to get involved in church work. We will let someone else do it. We belong to the "Society of Onlookers." "Wake me up when it's over," we say. "Don't get me involved. It takes time and effort and energy to do church work. Let somebody else do it."

Could apathy be the reason the church seems to have so little power today? Someone has said that the power of the church today is about as loud as the hiccups of a butterfly. This sad commentary is often true when we observe how few people will serve in the congregation of a local church. There is a need for you to find your place of service and ministry in your church. You and I affect the power of our congregations.

Jesus Christ did not say that we would know his disciples because they were members of such and such a church. He said we would know his disciples "by their fruits," by the way they live and serve. The writer of the book of James noted that "faith without works is dead." The church at Sardis that John wrote about in the book of Revelation had the form of faith but no substance. They had a name for being alive but were dead (Rev 3:1). Who knows what their church was like? Maybe at one time it had been a vital, powerful church, but now it was all structure, all organization, with no vitality or life, no sense of the aliveness or power of Christ's Spirit.

Too often we can become apathetic as a congregation. We expect somebody else to do everything for us. We wait for somebody else to pay for the building; somebody else to teach our children; somebody else to sing in the choir. We expect somebody else to usher; somebody else to visit; somebody else to carry on the work of the congregation—not "me." Let somebody else do it. I will stand back and be detached and uncommitted. I will receive, not give.

Several years ago, a minister tried something sensational to see if he could wake up his congregation that seemed to be very much asleep. One Sunday morning he placed a casket at the front of the sanctuary and invited each member of the congregation to come by and view the deceased. As they came by and looked into the casket, they saw a mirror in the bottom. Later that morning, he preached a sermon in which he noted that their congregation was dying because of the person each one saw reflected in the mirror in the casket. Each one was responsible for the life of the church. Granted, no one can keep a church going on sensationalism, but there is a point in what the preacher was saying. Each of us is significant and important in the church's work. We are called to be involved, not just to be spectators.

Dag Hammarskjold was correct when he said the path to holiness necessarily leads through action. "Faith without works is dead." We cannot expect to find a greater, more different, newer, or more complete insight from God when we never open ourselves to God. If we do not take advantage of the opportunities to serve God that are given to us in this moment, in this hour, this week, this month, this year, how can we look for more? God is constantly seeking to give us new insights and new truths, but most of us hold back or remain uninvolved and are not able to receive the gifts God desires to give us.

God Could Not Care More

Would you not also agree with me that the central teaching of the Christian faith is that the eternal God could not care more? When God came in Jesus Christ, this was the great declaration of God's love and concern for humanity. "For God so loved the world that he gave his only begotten son" (John 3:16). God didn't want to remain remote, detached, or uninvolved. We do not worship a God who is distant from us—a God who is uncaring or apathetic to our needs. In Jesus Christ, we see revealed a God who has come among us to show us love, grace, and care. The incarnation reveals the God who cares supremely for God's children. God became flesh and dwelt among us. The same God who came in Jesus Christ and laid down his life that we might find life continues to show us love and mercy through the centuries in Jesus Christ our Lord.

Within the Scriptures, we find that blood is a significant symbol for the Hebrew people. We read in the Hebrews 9:22, for example, that "without the shedding of blood there is no remission of sin." Blood was symbolic to the Jews of the outpouring of life. The ancient Hebrews offered animals as sacrifices to God to symbolize the outpouring of their lives in commitment to God. Jesus Christ's blood was shed; it was the outpouring of his life. His life was the life of God laid down for us. We participate and share in the life he brings as we are drawn to him. The cross of Jesus Christ that was set in place on the hillside in Palestine was not just an isolated moment revealing God's love. That event was not the only time in history when God has been loving. The cross of Jesus Christ shows us the eternal love of God, the sacrificial nature and extent of God's love. But God has always been loving. God has always reached out to love God's children. Jesus Christ was "the lamb slain from the foundation of the world" (Rev 13:8). In Christ, we see the heart of God that has been laid open, reaching out to God's children to say to them, "I love you. I care for you, and I want to give you the best in life." The cross on the hillside in ancient Israel was the external manifestation of the eternal love of God.

How many times have I heard a parent say when a child is ill, "Oh, how I wish I could bear that illness for them"? "I wish I could take that pain into myself." The cross of Christ is our acknowledgment of God bearing our pain. It is the external exemplification of God's love breaking into history. The cross is our way of knowing that God bears our pain. God bears our load; God lifts us up when we have fallen; God cares for us.

Christians Are Charged to Share the Good News

Most importantly, once we have experienced this love of God, if others are to know of it, then you and I are charged to live the kind of life that illustrates how we have walked with the Christ who revealed the God of love and grace. What are we to do? We hear the cries that come to us from the hungry, the needy, and those who long for clothing and shelter. Our ears and our eyes are bombarded by these needs. What shall we do?

Well, for one thing, *we can ignore them*. We can bury our heads in the paper or turn to another television station. We can take a walk or get more involved in some other kind of recreation. We can ignore the problems and needs of the world. We can pretend that they are not real. We can ignore the problems within our own families.

Or *we can rebel*. We can rebel against the problems. We can see all the problems in the world and say, "Well, that proves there is no God, doesn't it? If there were a God, he would do something about it." We can join those who have thrown up their hands and asked, "What is the point of it all? Let's just go our way." On the other hand, we could identify with those who have problems. We could simply become a part of the problem. We could create more problems with increased emphasis on sexual immorality, violence, and robbery as we make that way our way.

As adults, we sometimes *blame the younger generation* for most of the problems we encounter today involving sex and violence. Who puts sex and violence on television, the internet, and in the movies? It is not the kids but the adults. We have helped create the problems, and it seems that we continue to be a part of the problem. If there is to be an answer to these problems, it will require involvement from you and me. We have to decide to be a part of the answer and not a part of the problem.

Note the Supremacy of Love and Caring

Look closely at the thirteenth chapter of Paul's letter to the Corinthians. He wrote about the supremacy of love. He contrasted love with eloquence, prophecy, mystery, faith, charity, and even the sacrifice of one's own life. When we have the love of God in our life, we are patient, kind, generous, humble, courteous, unselfish, good-tempered, guileless, sincere, enduring, trusting, hoping, able to bear all things. Paul continues his description of love and states that love lasts. It is permanent, complete, and supreme. As William Baird has expressed it, "Faith is something we do, and hope is something we have; love belongs to the being of God."[1] When we are loving and when we are caring, we are more like God than at any other time in our lives. Clarence Jordan has translated some of the verses in 1 Corinthians 13 this way: "Love is all embracing, all trusting, all hoping, all enduring. Love never quits."[2] Love and care never stop and never give up because of difficulties. They rise up to meet the challenge and need. When we are unloving and uncaring, we are less like God. Substitute the word "care" for "love" in this passage and note how care can apply love in a special way. "The work of Christian realism in our time begins in worship and teaching," Robin Lovin writes, "remembering that even those who sing and pray with us may never have heard it except as an answer to problems they already knew they had. The gospel presents a harder truth: it calls us to be changed in a way that changes what we want."[3] Surely this is a call to love and care for others as Christ loves and cares for us.

Baron Friedrich von Hügel, a German philosopher, once wrote, "Caring is everything; nothing matters but caring." Was Socrates correct when he said, "Before a person can move the world, he must first be moved himself"? If you and I are going to make a difference in our church, community, city, or world, we must first be moved by care and love. God must touch our lives. Having been reconciled to God, Paul wrote, we have been called to a ministry of reconciliation —not to be spectators. We have now been called to be involved as God's children in the world. In the parable of the Good Samaritan, we read about two men, a priest and Levite, who passed by a man in need. They were spectators. They did not want to become involved. They walked on the far side away from human need. But the Good Samaritan cared. He loved and was willing to risk getting involved. In the parable of the Prodigal Son, we see one who cared only for himself. But when he came to his true self in his time of need, then he went back to his father. It was only when he got outside of himself that he found his real self. When we are concerned only with our immediate needs, then we never discover who we really are.

Several years ago, a boy rushed in his front door and told his father that he'd had an awful experience that day on the beach. He said, "Daddy, I saw a woman who was drowning in the ocean, and there were people all around her. She had gone down several times and had screamed for help, but none of those in their bathing suits in the ocean would go and help her. She went down several more times, and then finally a man who was fully dressed and who had been walking by on the sidewalk rushed down into the water and pulled her to safety. Daddy, nobody seemed to care." The father drew his son close to him and said, "Son, let me tell you something. Before you judge people too harshly, remember this. It takes great courage to care."

It does take courage to care, but caring is the essence of the Christian gospel. God cared so much for us that God came in God's Son

Jesus Christ that we might have life. This same God has called us to reach out to the hungry, the blind, the naked, the deaf—to all humanity—and touch them with our concern. God has told us that judgment will come according to the way we have cared for people. Judgment is realized in a cup of water given, a visit to those in jail, and bread for the hungry. May we learn to care for others even as God has cared supremely for us and continues to do so. We can't be spectators when we are in God's kingdom. God has recruited kingdom-builders. This calls us to rise up and be at work.

Chapter 13

Speaking a Distinct Word

1 Corinthians 14:1–19

Words. Words. Words. How quickly, easily, and carelessly they often come to our lips. Did you know that the average person speaks about thirty thousand words a day? This means that the average person speaks enough to write a short book. If our speaking were written down over a lifetime, each of us could fill up a good-sized library with books. There are over three thousand languages and dialects in the world. Words are vehicles that enable us to communicate with each other. Without words communication is almost impossible.

Words can be powerful. They can be helpful, incisive, and directing. Words can be used to bless or to curse. Words can praise or condemn. Words can encourage or discourage. Words can be said in anger or in love. Words can help or hinder. Words are powerful instruments in our mouths. We utilize a lot of words all the time. How do you and I use our words?

Word Problems

The Apostle Paul was no stranger to words. He knew a lot about words because he spoke a great deal and wrote several epistles. This passage from 1 Corinthians 14 is about a church that had word problems. Some of the words they were using in their worship were indistinct. The use of these words as a part of their worship was causing difficulties and divisions. Some had said, "I am for Apollos" or "I am for Paul" or "I am for Peter." Because of such words, the church divided into camps built around certain personalities. Then each camp began to talk about the other, as often happens when divisions take place. They soon began gossiping about each other. Paul reminded them that this harmed the church. Harsh words could be said quickly and easily, but this action could hurt the whole church.

In the small epistle of James (3:1-12), the tongue is described as a powerful instrument. The writer states that sometimes the tongue can be like poison. Words can poison another person's life due to their impact. After the Second World War, a large supply of Blue Cross Gas was left, and the English government did not know what to do with the poisonous gas. They thought at first that they would burn it. But the farmers nearby complained, "You can't do that. It will destroy all the vegetation." They suggested they would bury it in the ground, but environmentalists said, "You can't do that because it will destroy the underground water supply." Then they wondered if they might float it down the Rhine River into the ocean. But they quickly realized that they could not do that because it was too dangerous to try to move it down the river. Finally, they put the gas in a concrete box and buried it deep within one of the moors and hoped that nobody would find it for thirty years.

Isn't it amazing how quickly and sometimes easily we can manufacture poison and then not know what to do with it once we have it? Poison can enter our lives and quickly and easily destroy us, and often we have no control over what happens. Paul's letter to the Corinthian church attempted to offer an antidote to the poison created by division.

Judgmental Words

Paul also wrote about the words the church had used to judge others when they were divided into these camps. Some of them even criticized Paul himself. They didn't understand, for example, why he had not come to visit them sooner or why he had done certain things. Harshly and quickly, their words of judgment came against him and others. Most of us can relate to this. Before we realize it, words rush to our lips and we have verbalized them, and we see them dig deeply into the life of another person, hurting them. We perhaps cannot recall those words once we say them. The act is done.

One time a woman came to Francis of Assisi and told him that she had spread a false rumor about another woman in her community, and she was deeply sorrowful for what she had done. She wondered what she could do to repent. Francis asked her to bring him a pillow. She brought him one, and he took a knife and cut the pillow open and threw the feathers up into the air. The wind caught the feathers and blew them in every direction. Then he said to the woman, "Go now and gather the feathers for the pillow." She tried but soon came back and told him that it was impossible. He then told her, "Remember when you spread false rumors that it is impossible to go back and undo what you have done." Paul knew what improperly directed words could do within the church. He called the Corinthians not to sit in judgment upon one another or look down on others. Paul's caution reminds us of the words of Jesus: "Judge not that you be not judged" (Matt 7:1).

Self-centeredness

Paul also attempted to confront the self-centeredness of many within the Corinthian church. Some of them seemed to be saying, "Ah, look at me. I am a superior Christian to you because I have more ecstatic speech. I speak in tongues and you do not. Therefore, that makes me a superior Christian."

I am astounded at those who want to take what Paul calls the lesser of the gifts and elevate it to the position of a superior gift. Many individuals who claim to have a second blessing look down on everybody else as a kind of third-class Christian because they cannot speak in an ecstatic tongue or they have not had a "special blessing." If ecstatic speech is so high in the church, it is interesting that the Lord Jesus Christ himself never spoke in tongues. The one who brought the Spirit to us was not a tongue speaker but instead condemned "babbling." It is also interesting that it is only within this epistle that Paul deals with tongues speaking. This issue divided the most corrupt church to which Paul ever wrote. Paul reminded them that ecstatic speech was the lowest gift of all. Among God's many gifts, it was low on the list because it was selfish. It only satisfied the one using it. It did not help another person.

The church where tongues speaking was a problem was laden with immorality, lawsuits, marital problems, divisions, and quarrels. This was the church where people did not believe in the resurrection. They quarreled at the Lord's Supper table, and some got drunk and refused to wait for others who arrived late. The church was riddled with emotions that had been at the center of their pagan worship before they became Christians. Paul cautioned them against putting something that should be private and personal into public worship. "Cool it" and "control it" seem to be key words of advice from Paul.

In one church where I pastored, a woman was involved in the glossolalia movement. She claimed to be able to speak in tongues. But never in all the nine years that I was pastor there did she attempt to introduce it into the life of the church, convert other people to it, or say to them that unless they had the gift, they were not as good a Christian as she was. She used her gift in a private way that edified her and nourished her and the small group that occasionally met with her. Paul says this kind of use of tongues speaking is acceptable. But a problem arises when any group, no matter what kind of speech it may use, brings its approach into the church and tries to make its way paramount, declaring that people who do not engage in it are not as close to God.

While the Corinthian church struggled with many divisive issues, the Jerusalem church, the church on which God poured the Spirit as they gathered at Pentecost, was also the church that was most united and had a warm fellowship. This church preached a clear word, and thousands were won to Christ. When God's Spirit came upon this church, the results were positive. On the other hand, the Corinthian church was divided, confused, and often immoral. Do not mistake indistinct speech for the highest gift. Let it have its place in private worship, but do not involve it in corporate worship where other people are not aided or edified by what an individual is saying or doing. The New Testament gives other signs that a person is filled with the Spirit. Tongues speaking is not an essential or superior gift for the Christian life.

Guidelines for a Distinct Word

Paul offers guidelines on how to speak a distinct word for Christ. He offers at least four suggestions, and I enumerate these briefly here.

Build Up the Church

First, Paul says we should use our speech to build up the church. We are challenged to build it up and edify it so that the church might grow and increase in the knowledge and grace of Christ. We do not want to hurt it or distort it by our words. Whenever you want to say something about an individual or group, ask yourself several questions.

1. Is It True?

How do you know it is true and not a rumor? Are you really going to build up your congregation, your church, or an individual by what you are saying?

It was said of one person that he always seemed to have a keen sense of *rumor*. Some people seem to pick up quickly anything that is rumored and fan the slightest bit of smoke into a raging fire. They assume that where there is smoke there is always fire. There were those who said Jesus was a drunk and a glutton. There were those who said he was guilty of blasphemy. There were those who said he sought to become an earthly king. Was it true in the case of Jesus that where there was smoke there was fire? Just because somebody spread those rumors about Jesus, did that make them true? Of course not. Ask yourself: Is it true? Have I heard it correctly? Sometimes we hear things in strange ways. Our mind plays tricks on us.

One of the Charlie Brown stories is about this problem. Charlie Brown walks into the living room with his baseball glove in his hand. He is rubbing some oil in it, and he says to Lucy and Sally, who are watching television, "I am going to rub some Neet-Foot Oil into my glove and then put it away for the winter." Lucy says, "That's good." In a few minutes, Linus comes in and asks, "Where is Charlie Brown?" Lucy, not looking away from the TV, says, "I don't know. He said something about how neat it is to wear gloves on your feet in the wintertime."

Is it true? Have you really heard it correctly? Does it build up the person? Does it build up the congregation?

2. Is It Necessary?

A second question to ask if you want to say something about someone else is whether it is helpful to say it. Does it in some way help another individual, encourage him, build her up, or help the congregation if you share it? Suppose somebody texts you in anger. Do you share that text with everybody? Is it really necessary to do that? That person may have texted when he was down or angry and simply wanted to unload his feelings. Is it necessary to share it with others? We don't need to tell every single thing we know or feel.

3. Is It Helpful?

A final question when deciding whether to say something is to ask whether it is helpful. Does it really help a congregation or a person for you to say or do those things? Does it only help you? Does it make you look better? Does it puff you up so that somehow you get some glory?

A woman was talking to a friend one day and told her that her neighbors next door were having tremendous marital problems. "They are the talk of our neighborhood. Everybody is taking sides," she said. "They are either on his side or on her side." The friend said, "And I suppose there are a few eccentric individuals who are minding their own business?" Is it helpful to get into the middle of something about which you and I may not have the correct information? Does it build up the body of Christ? This is Paul's first suggestion. Do our words build up the church, or do they hurt it? He says again and again in this passage that our words, our conversation, and our actions should be expressed to build up, strengthen, and fortify the church.

Use Words Intelligently

Second, Paul says that our words must be intelligible. It is easy for us to slip into using confusing terms; even theologians and philosophers do that. Talk to seminary students about some of their courses and they will tell you about professors who speak in a specialized theological language that is an unknown tongue to their students. Almost any kind of discipline or special vocation, like law, medicine, accounting, insurance, or science, has its own particular language. Sometimes we can't understand what an individual is saying when she uses her discipline's vocabulary. Another person in that same discipline may understand it, but an outsider will not.

Paul says that tongues speaking may satisfy an individual, but it doesn't help other people. He notes to the Corinthians that if he had come to their church preaching in "tongues," they would not have understood the gospel message of Christ so they could become Christians.

If musical instruments like the trumpet, flute, and lyre have an indistinct sound, Paul asked, how can they be helpful? The trumpet was used to guide soldiers in battle. The lyre called people to worship. These instruments had a distinct purpose. Paul also reminded them that if one could not speak the foreign language used by another person, then that language would not make any sense to him. It would sound like gibberish. We need to be able to communicate with one another. Our speech has to be intelligible and understandable for that to happen. At Pentecost, the people heard the gospel in the "tongues" of their own languages. The tongues were intelligible and normal speech, not unintelligible and ecstatic. Paul also instructed the Corinthians that their experience of worship should not be purely emotional. Some people were caught up in an ecstatic language and had become so involved in it that they thought it was the only way to address God. But Paul reminded them that this speech only satisfied themselves.

Even today, many people want religion to be on what I call the "goosebump level." "Do you really feel it, brother?" they ask. Religion is not just a feeling. Too many people think that if they don't feel something, they haven't received anything. We may get psyched up emotionally at a football or basketball game, but there is a radical difference between those kinds of emotions and religious feelings. Some people have never learned to make the distinction. Religion is not just emotional. I am not saying that emotion is not involved. It is. Who wants a religion devoid of all emotions? Our religion, however, is not based only on whether it makes us feel good and have warm feelings. Love is not just "a warm, gooey feeling" either. Too often people identify this Valentine kind of approach to love with authentic religion. Religion is not just emotion; there must also be understanding.

Interpret Ecstatic Speech

Third, Paul advised the Corinthians that ecstatic speech requires interpretation. If a person speaks in an ecstatic language (glossolalia), there must be someone to interpret for them, or nobody else gets anything out of it. Glossolalia satisfies only the individual who is doing it and not the other people who listen. And really, all of our religion demands interpretation. That is the reason we have Sunday school classes, small group studies, and preaching services. There has to be constant interpretation and translation of the gospel so people can understand it in their own language, place, and time. Too much of our faith doesn't make sense to others and demands interpretation and clarification. It is amazing how indistinct our religion can be, especially the theological words we use to describe it.

When I was living in Bristol, Virginia, I served on the board of directors for the YMCA. Frank Marney served as director there for many years. We were in conversation once with Frank after he had retired. He was in his mid-eighties then, but his mind was just as sharp and alert as ever. He was telling Emily, my wife, and me how he had begun the camp that the Y had built about fifty years ago. He said it was located in a backwoods place in Tennessee, and they hired some rural farmers who had never been into the city. The farmers had finished part of the construction of the camp. Mr. Marney came down one Friday and said to them, "Well, men, it looks like you are going to finish this by tomorrow. On Monday we can start the gymnasium. I am really pleased with what you have done."

When he came back the next day, one of the men who acted as spokesman for this group of carpenters came over to him and said, "Mr. Marney, I hate to tell you, but all of the men have decided they are going to quit." Frank asked, "Why, what's wrong?" The man said, "Well, we just decided we've got to quit." "Come over here," Frank said, "and let's sit down under this tree. You must tell me. Obviously, I have said something to offend you, and I need to know what I can do to help because I need you as workers. I must have you. Tell me what is wrong. I can take it if you have some criticism. Just tell me." The man looked at him and stared and didn't say a word. "Mr. Marney," he finally said, "we all consider ourselves right good builders, but we don't know what a gymnasium is, and we can't build something when we don't know what it is, so we are going to quit." Mr. Marney was a sharp fellow and said, "I'll tell you what. I made a mistake. We are not going to build a gymnasium. We are going to build a great big barn, and I know you know how to build a great big barn. That is what we are going to do." "Sure, we'll come back," the man responded. "We know how to build a barn, but we don't know what a gymnasium is."

Communication is essential for action. Our inability to understand each other can be devastating. These farmers needed somebody to interpret for them. In the church, there must be someone to interpret for people what the grace of God means so they can respond to it. A part of the church's function is to translate the gospel for others.

Offer an Encouraging Word

Fourth, Paul wrote to encourage the people. Encouragement builds up the church. Each of us has a deep need in our lives for words of support, undergirding, and affirmation. If we leave church and go into life on a flat tire, we can't get very far, can we? We need a Christian faith that is more than just rolling on three wheels with one side that is deflated and uninspired. The impact of the spirit of Christ on us is inspiring. People long for support. Our words should come to others as uplifting words and not downgrading words. Our words can be inspiring and not rejecting. They should come as words of hope and not despair. Words can be sustaining when life seems to be collapsing. Our words can warm another person's spirit when they are feeling blue. A church should encourage one another, Paul says. Let's undergird each other with that kind of encouragement.

Make Love the Aim

Finally, Paul instructs the church to make love their aim. Love should be at the center of everything you and I do in our speech and action. My goal is not what I can get out of it, what it can do for me, but what I can do to express the love of Christ that I have already experienced. Let's make love our aim. When love is our aim, then we will reach out and strengthen people and not hurt them. We will encourage them and not discourage them. When love is our aim, we will lift up another person when they have fallen and not crush them down more. When a person makes a mistake, if love is our aim, we will reach over and help them up. When love is our aim and a person is grieving, we will comfort and sustain them. We will strive to strengthen, not weaken. When a person feels alienated, if love is our aim, we will draw them back to the fellowship and embrace them. When love is our aim, we are understanding. We know that people who come to understand, and people who understand know how to love. This is a part of the authentic gospel because God is love. Anyone who has understood this love will seek to be loving in all that is said and done.

A man was talking with a friend one day, and some angry words came bursting out. The man backed away from his friend and said, "Well, I really didn't mean that. I'm sorry. I didn't mean it." His friend reached over and got a Coke and shook the bottle hard before he uncapped it. You know what happens to a bottle of Coke when you do that. Suddenly it spewed all over both of them. "Let me tell you something," he exclaimed. "Nothing came out of this Coke bottle that wasn't within it. What came out of you in anger was a reflection of what is inside of you."

When you and I spew anger, vindictiveness, hostility, and hatred on others, it reveals what is inside us. We simply cannot say we don't mean it. We must put the right ingredients inside of us so that, in difficult situations, the right things will come out of us. It is easy to say "I didn't mean it," but it is far better to seek something within us that fills our lives with love, compassion, grace, and understanding. Learn, Paul says, to speak a distinctive word because it is the word of Christ. It is the word of love. It is the word of upbuilding. It is the word of encouragement. It is the word that is intelligent. It is the word that is loving and sustaining.

Tolstoy wrote a story about two women who came to a counselor for help one day. They both suffered from a sense of unforgiveness. One of the women had committed adultery and wanted to find forgiveness. The other woman did not know exactly what she had done, but she felt like she had made a lot of little mistakes and wanted to find forgiveness. The wise counselor in Tolstoy's story told the woman who had committed adultery to go to a field nearby and bring back the largest stone she could find. He told the woman who had committed the smaller acts but did not know what they were to bring back a lot of small stones. When they returned, he told them to go back and place the stones where they had found them. It was easy for the woman who had found the large stone to go back and place it in its hole. "You are aware of your great sin," the counselor told her. "Just as you knew where to return the big rock, so by your admission you have freed yourself from your guilt. God has forgiven you. So now forgive yourself and profit from the experience." But the woman who had gathered the small stones did not know where she had picked up many of them, and she could not return them. The counselor said, "You do not have any big sins but many small ones which make you unhappy. As *you* lost track of where you picked up the small stones, so, too, you are unaware of your faults. Many small sins can be worse than one big one. Do not judge others; you have enough to do improving your own life."[1]

The good news of the gospel is that anyone who has committed a big sin or small sins can find forgiveness from God and begin anew. Once we have experienced the power of the love of God in our lives, once this spirit has penetrated us, then we can go forth to love in god's name. If love is the central ingredient in all our living, then others will feel it in the contact they have with us every day. Make love your aim. Speak a distinct word so that others can see clearly that Jesus Christ lives within your life.

Chapter 14

The Congregation at Worship

1 Corinthians 14:26-33, 37-40

The placard on the bus read, "In this day, every American needs to find God. Go to church on Sunday." Underneath it someone had written, "I went but he was not there." It's obvious that there are a lot of folks who feel that God is not there, or they have not found God in church—because a lot of folks do not go much at all. In the United States, a "Christian" nation, only about twenty percent of Americans go to church on a typical Sunday. In England only about ten percent of people go to church on Sunday. All we have to do is look around, even on a great Sunday, and see that only fifty percent or less of church members attend worship on a regular basis. So many people feel that they have either missed God in church or that it is not very important to go.

Significance of Worship

Archaeologists tell us that when they dig up ancient ruins, they find three basic things no matter the civilization: a prison, an altar, and a cemetery. People sin. They worship. And they die. In some way, all civilizations have found that worship is supposed to be central to their way of life. But as generations pass, other things appear to be more significant, more important, and more at the forefront of people's lives than worship.

A small girl came to her mother one day and said, "Mother, you know that vase that has been passed on from one generation to the other?" The mother said, "Oh, yes, I know. It is one of my prized possessions." "Well, this new generation has dropped it." Where is worship in the lives of many folks? They seemed to have dropped it. Somehow God seems to be missing, unimportant, or unrelated to their lives.

The biblical writers did not spend much time trying to argue why people should worship. They simply assumed that those who loved God would worship. They assumed that those with a relationship to God would come, bow down, and worship before God because they saw it as a part of one's very being and existence.

Christ Opens Our Worship Directly to God

Paul reminds the Corinthians in his letter that they gather to worship because of what Christ has done for them. In ancient Israelite times, when the people went to the temple to worship, the holy of holies was hidden behind a veil that separated the people from the presence of God. Only once a year was the high priest allowed to go into that holy of holies. The Scriptures tell us that when Jesus Christ died, the temple veil was rent, torn in two, so that people were able to have direct access to God. As T. H. Robinson says, "The path to the inner heart of God is now open."[1] Through Jesus Christ, we can enter directly and boldly into the presence of God and worship.

The writer of the letter to the Hebrews (10:19-25) tells us that Jesus Christ is our high priest. We do not need other priests. Christ is not only the high priest but is himself the offering to God. He is both the sacrifice and the one who makes the sacrificial way open to God. He literally is the way. He has made the way, opening for us the path into the very presence of God. He has bridged the gap that separated people from God and has brought us directly into God's presence. He has overcome the separation. In ancient times, every sacrifice had to have the sprinkling of blood upon it, but the writer tells us here that through the blood of Jesus Christ we have been cleansed. Now we can come directly and immediately into the presence of God and worship. Every Sunday, then, is an Easter cele-bration. The early Christians made a dramatic move from honoring the Sabbath on Saturday to observing it on Sunday, the Resurrection

Day of Christ. This was a bold move. The Christians came boldly into the presence of God.

Approach the Presence of God

In our worship we seek to approach the presence of God, declaring that God is at the center of our worship. It is God that we adore. God is the One who has great majesty and power. God is the One who is high and lifted up—the exalted One. We come not so much to study God as to be dazzled by God's presence. We come in a sense of awe. Through Scripture, prayer, hymns, and preaching, we are confronted by the majesty and righteousness of God. Sometimes if we enter a dark room and someone else is there, we say to them, "Switch on the light so I might see." Coming to worship is an attempt to switch on the light so we might see the presence of God among us. God is the central focus in our worship.

The word "worship" comes from an ancient Anglo-Saxon word that means "worth-ship." Worship is ascribing worth to someone or something. We have ascribed great worth to God as the One worthy of our highest worship. The Hebrew word for worship means "to bow down or prostrate oneself before God." The Greek word for worship literally means "to kiss toward." It is bowing with a sense of reverence and affection.

Worship Is Something We Do for God

As we gather to worship in the name of God, we need to remember that worship is not so much something God does for us as something we do for God. You raise the wrong question if you ask somebody, "Did you get anything from the worship service?" We do not *get something* from worship. We are supposed to *give something*. We come to glorify God, not to edify ourselves. We gather to give something to God—our praise and adoration. We come before God because of what God has done for us. We worship even when we do not feel like it. We do not worship just when we are in the mood for it or are happy and content. We worship because it is something worthy to do for the One to whom we direct our allegiance and our lives. We do not pay our rent, car loan, or house payment just when we feel like it. We do not buy groceries only when we feel like it. All of these things need to be done because they are a part of life. We come to worship and bow before God because God is worthy of our praise. So let us worship God and forget the roast in the oven for a while. Let us forget the bills; forget the entanglements of our business world; forget the economic and world problems. Let us simply come worship God. Let us focus on God. In these moments, let us give God our lives and attention. Let our worship pour forth with enthusiasm and radiance as we sense the power of God's presence among us.

Recalling Memories

Worship is also a recalling of memories. It is like looking through a scrapbook or a picture album and reminiscing. Worship takes us back to the place of remembrance where we met God. Worship is a time of going back through the pages of our lives in this church and other churches. It is linking our lives with Abraham, Isaac, and Jacob. It is joining with the generations from Matthew, Mark, and Paul. It is a time of recalling memories of when others have met God and when we have met God. It is remembering times when we have sung hymns and praised God. Worship is not just entertainment. One of the great corruptions of worship in our time has come from television evangelism, which often equates worship and entertainment. Worship from this perspective focuses primarily on whether it makes us feel good when we get together. To these folks, worship is something that is sentimental, entertaining, or clever.

I recall watching a couple of young people singing one time in church. They were singing about the love of God, but they spent the whole time looking adoringly into each other's eyes. The young boy and girl seemed more interested in each other than in God. Too many churches have bought the show business approach to church and have confused entertainment with worship. Let us come with a sense of the awesomeness of the holy God of the universe and bow before God's presence. Let us sense God's majesty. Let us approach God aware of the radiance and the power of who God is and, whether we are entertained or not, remember that worship is something we do for God and not so much something that God does for us.

Orderly Worship

As we approach God in worship, let us do it with order. Paul admonishes the Corinthians (1 Cor 14:40), "Let all things be done decently and in order." Baptists and some other evangelical groups are not noted for their great order in worship. Sometimes we can be sloppy in our congregational worship. We need to go back to the ancient Scriptures and learn what authentic worship is. In worship we need to be open to sense the breath of God blowing upon us. We should not be confined to rigid molds of worship but remain open to let the freshness of God's Spirit enter us. God's creativity can warm the coals of our spirits and bring new fire into our lives as our worship is ignited by the power of God's presence among us. Let us have order but not rigidity. Direction and care are important for corporate worship. Let us be experimental and probe to find new avenues and opportunities in our worship. As your church attempts to make a minor change here and there, I hope you do not say, "We have always done it that way." We may need to study to see how others have worshiped God in order to discover new ways to sense the power of God's presence as we worship with "order."

Holiness of God

Let us gather to worship with a sense of awareness that we come before the holiness of God. Isaiah spoke about the God he worshiped in the temple, who was high and lifted up. We should never just stumble into the presence of God on Sunday; we should come with an awareness that we are approaching the presence of the holy God of the universe. Isaiah experienced in his worship the might of a God whose robe edge filled the great temple. His sense of God's height, the God above all, and God's majesty were almost overwhelming. Isaiah's faith became alive for him in this experience of worship (Isa 6:1-8). Isaiah would have understood the small book written by J. B. Phillips with the title *Your God Is Too Small*. God is the great God before whom we fall down and exclaim, "Holy, holy, holy is your name." God is the Lord of hosts. God is in the place of our worship. Do not miss God's presence. God is present! Bow before God.

Praise God

We gather also with praise on our lips. The voice of the organ calls us to praise God for what God has done and to affirm God's good gifts to us. We praise God when things have gone well and when things have gone poorly. We praise God in the time of birth and in the time of death and with assurance: "Blessed be the name of the Lord." We lift up our voices and sing with a sense of enthusiasm and joy. Refusing to sing is to sin against the body of the congregation, because it is part of what we do in unity together to express our joy unto God. We can all make a joyful noise. The Scriptures do not say that we all have to sing well, but at the great sound of the organ, let praise go forth among us as we lift our voices to God.

C. S. Lewis once said that he got tired of people always saying we should praise God. He could not understand it. He wondered if God were the great egotist who had to have people always talking about him. Gradually he began to realize that it was not a question of egotism but of love. If we love somebody, we want to express that love to them. A sports enthusiast wants to express their feelings when the team scores a touchdown or makes a basket. An artist must express their talent on the canvas. If we genuinely love God, praise will come forth. It is a part of our very being.

I heard about a man who received an opportunity to go horseback riding on a beautiful stallion trained by a rather religious person. As he got on the back of the horse, the owner told him that there were two basic commands for this horse. When you want him to stop you have to say, "Amen." And when you want him to go you say, "Praise the Lord." The man went galloping off on the horse and was enjoying his ride until suddenly the horse started racing toward a cliff. He began to say, "Whoa, halt, stop." He could not think of the right word to call the horse to a halt. Right at the edge of the cliff he remembered the word for stop and yelled, "Amen." The horse stopped in the nick of time. The man was so overjoyed that he said,

"Praise the Lord." Sometimes, when we are honest, we fear that if we praise the Lord we might be jumping off the cliff. It's worth the risk, don't you think? As we lift our voices in praise to God, others will hopefully detect our sensitivity to God's power and presence.

A Time of Prayer and Confession

Let us worship God with a sense of prayer and confession. Notice that Isaiah came into the holy presence of God, and he was immediately made aware of his sinfulness. We come before God as Christians saved by God's grade yet aware that we are still sinners. We come to confess our sins. Isaiah experienced the purging and cleansing power that came from the presence of God through the symbol of the hot coal on his lips. This reminds us that forgiveness of sins is not easy. Forgiveness is sometimes painful as well as cleansing. We come to God to confess our sins and experience God's forgiveness as we gather together.

Worship affords us a time in which we can wrap the mantle of silence around ourselves. We need zones of silence so we will have opportunities to confess our sins and to experience the power of God as we worship together.

Proclamation or Prophecy

Paul reminds us to worship God with a sense of proclamation. We gather in worship knowing that in this place, God's word will go forth through song, prayers, preaching, the reading of the Scriptures, and silence. God's word will be proclaimed among us so that God's Spirit can come into our midst, challenging our styles of living and our understanding of life and lifting us up to be more than we are. The Word of God walks through the written and proclaimed word to confront us with our sins and our need to respond to God's grace. God's word will be proclaimed—"Thus saith the Lord"—as we seek to direct our lives in God's way.

Giving of an Offering

Let us worship together with an offering. As the psalmist says, "Bring an offering and come into my courts" (Ps 96:8). Does God need our money? No. God does not need it. But our money and our possessions are symbolic of who and what we are. We bring them into the presence of God because they are a sign of our commitment to God. We give a bit of ourselves through our money and possessions and declare through our giving that materialism is not our chief end. I seek to use my material possessions in ways that glorify God.

Prepare for Worship

Let us approach God in our worship together in praise and affirmation. As we come to a time of togetherness, I hope that we will learn to do some preparation for worship. I know it is hard to prepare. We often stay out too late on Saturday night and do not get enough sleep. We then come rushing into the service. For Jewish people, the Sabbath begins on Friday night, and they use that time to prepare for the next day's worship. Most of us walk into the church service without any preparation or thought, and we expect the ministers and choir to make worship happen for us. When it does not, we say, "Oh, haven't they done poorly today?" You and I have a part in preparation. After we arrive in the church sanctuary, we need to pause and prepare to put ourselves in tune with God. It is good to talk and converse with friends when we first arrive, but when we hear the voice of the organ, the time of meditation begins. Use that time to focus your thoughts on God and prepare for God's presence among your congregation. Some of us think worship is like the ads we see: "Lose 30 pounds in 30 days," or "Learn to speak French in 30 days." Do you really believe those ads? I hope you do not. It takes more time, preparation, and discipline to learn a language or to lose weight. We also need to have discipline in preparing ourselves for worship.

Active Involvement

Let us worship with participation through everything that is being done, whether it is the hymns, the call to worship, the prayers, the litanies, the affirmations, or the sermon. Everything calls for us to participate in what is happening in the service. As the Danish theologian Søren Kierkegaard once said, people often think that the preacher and the choir are supposed to be the chief actors in worship, staging a performance for the people in the congregation. But that is not true. All of us are involved in worship. God is the chief actor as God meets us in worship. The ministers and the choir are just the prompters who point us toward God so that each of us can sense the power of God's presence among us.

The writer of Hebrews says we should approach God in worship and then go forth with a sense of our beliefs incorporated in our lives so that they can direct us in how to live. Our beliefs give direction and meaning to our lives. Our origin and destiny are in God, and we have a deep hunger within us that pulls us back to the God who made us. When people cut themselves off from worship, they begin to sever the tie that enables them to have focus, direction, and meaning for life. We need to climb up the hill of worship so we can capture a greater glimpse of the way we can live when we have been enriched by the presence and power of God.

Paul directs the Corinthians to do all things in worship "to build up" the church. He calls them to find a sense of the high values to which God is calling them. Worship reminds us of the high values in life. It calls us to set our priorities right and to put first things first. Our focus is not merely on an individual's wants or desire in worship but on what enriches the whole community of faith. "Private devotion has its place: but it is not as important as public devotion which builds up the entire group," William Orr and James Arthur Walther write as they interpret Paul's injunction to the Corinthians. They continue, "The life of the church is more important than the religious development or expression of a single individual."[2] Each worshiper should participate and contribute their involvement with respect to others in their part in the service of worship. This should be done to encourage one another. We seek to enrich one another in our worship and "build up" one another and inspire goals, values, and means that enrich the whole body. Self-centeredness or selfishness have no place in our desire to worship God. As we have worshiped together, we get a new focus on what should have first place in our lives. We are a community of faith, bound to one another by faith in Jesus Christ as Lord. Worship reminds us of the most important values and ideals to which we should give our highest allegiance. God is worthy of my praise, and out of this adoration, my ethical living will follow. Having worshiped God, unworthy motives should be far from my desire.

The story goes that the *Titanic* was sinking, a wealthy man named Arthur Godfrey Peuchen left his many financial documents behind and took three oranges into the lifeboat instead. Isn't it strange that when a crisis comes, we begin to get our priorities right? Worship directs us to examine our luggage. Worship calls us together so that we can get our values and priorities right. And then we go into the world to live the kind of life that reflects that we have been in the presence of God.

Encourage One Another

Paul wrote to encourage the Corinthian church, and after we have worshiped, we also should encourage one another. Let us take heart with one another and support one another. Worship is not an isolated event. Worship is not just for us individually, as important as that may be, but we gather to share in each other's lives. Worship and our daily living are tied together. Our living is bound up with our worship, and our worship is linked with our daily walk. We leave our place of worship to go into the world to express concern for all of life. Real worship invades our business, home, and recreation—all of life. People must not see us gathering to worship on Sunday and then living an entirely different kind of life that denies the worship act the rest of the week. When we have worshiped God, worship should break into all of our being, and we need to encourage one another to live the kind of life that Christ would have us live as God's people in the world.

John Sherrill wrote about an experience he had when he decided he would join his church choir. He had not been in the choir for a long time, and as he began to sing, he became aware that he was not producing the tones he needed. Some of us do not have to join the choir to realize that! In the choir, he was sitting next to a man with a tremendous bass voice. Sitting next to this man helped John's singing tremendously, and after practice he mentioned to the man how much his singing had meant to him. The man said, "If that helped, I'll show you something even better next week." The next week when they gathered for choir practice, Bill Brogan whispered to him, "Lean into me." "What?" John said. "Put your weight on me," Bill said. John leaned back until his shoulder blade was resting against Bill's chest. He could feel the resonances of the music coming through Bill's body penetrating his own, and John said that it was amazing the difference that experience made in his own ability to sing.

Let us lean into each other. In a worshiping community, we do not try to go it alone; we lean on each other. We draw strength from each other and begin to understand what it means to be the body of Christ. We are God's people who draw strength and encouragement from each other. Individually and together, we lean into the strength we draw from God. A great symbol for worship might be Jacob's ladder. It extends up into heaven and then the angels descend. This ladder, as it extends upward, might symbolize our message to God: our prayers, praise, and offerings. Horton Davies says that the descending angels might symbolize God's messages to us through the proclaimed and written word.[3] As we gather for worship, let us approach God through the power of what Jesus Christ has done for us. Let our worship be so powerful and real that we will go from it into the world to live differently because we have worshiped together.

Chapter 15

Jesus's Resurrection: The Foundation of the Church

1 Corinthians 15:1–22

It has always been interesting to me that, whereas Christmas seems to turn the modern world on its head with everyone preparing months in advance in a flurry of activity, Easter does not stir much excitement in the lives of people today. Easter seems to whimper in, and most people scarcely notice its coming. If it is remembered, what images come to mind—Easter bunnies, egg hunts, new clothes, new hats, vacation time, and spring flowers? Easter comes and goes without much regard. In many places, only a handful of people attend special Easter services during "Holy Week" or on Maundy Thursday or Good Friday. We do not seem to realize that there would be no Christmas celebration without Easter. Easter was the first church holiday—not Christmas. Easter brought the church into existence.

Ernest Campbell, a former minister at Riverside Church in New York City, was confronted by a woman in his congregation at the church door following the Easter service. "Where were the trumpets?" she asked. "Beg your pardon?" he responded. "Where were the trumpets?" she continued. "We always have trumpets on Easter morning in our service." Where are the trumpets? Where are the resounding hallelujahs within the hearts and in the voices of Christians? Where are the shouts of praise and affirmation? "He is risen!" Why are our tongues silent, our voices muted, and no song employed?

The Fear of Death

Is it because many of us, even those in the churches, do not really believe the news of Easter? If we are honest, we have to admit that the fear of death is still our paramount fear. Many studies indicate that this is still true.[1] Death is the underlying fear of all people. Many are perplexed, disturbed, confused, and uncertain about the possibility of life after death. Job's question, "If a person dies, will he live again?" is contemporary humanity's question. Many today feel that any belief in life after death is only a fantasy, a pipe dream, or wishful thinking. Our materialistic scientific world does not seem to make belief in life after death plausible or possible.

Many years ago, Ernest Poole wrote a novel titled *The Harbor*. One of the characters in the story was an impatient and determined reformer who looked with disdain on history. "History," he once observed, "is just news from a graveyard." Ah! That is the Christian affirmation at Easter, is it not? History is news from a particular graveyard. The graveyard where they buried Jesus Christ was not the end because he is risen!

The Strange Word "Resurrection"

Resurrection is a word that still leaves us uncomfortable today, even after hearing it for two thousand years within the Christian community. The word "resurrection," however, was just as strange to the Corinthians to whom Paul wrote centuries ago. The Stoics believed that a person needed to be brave and accept death as the natural end of life. The Epicureans believed that life should be enjoyed to the fullest now because there was nothing beyond this life. Some Greeks believed that there was a spark in the soul that lived on, but that spark was not the real essence of personality. It was not the real person who survived. Paul challenged these beliefs with his startling message: "If you do not believe in the resurrection of Christ, you need to realize that the whole Christian faith tumbles!" To Paul, the resurrection of Christ was the foundation of the Christian faith.

The Early Christian Tradition

Paul begins this passage with a ringing declaration: "I am not giving you Corinthians something which is just my words. This message is not original with me; I am telling you what you have already received." Received from where? Paul's teaching was a part of the early Christian tradition that taught that Christ was crucified, died, was raised from the dead, and continues to live. At the time of Paul's writing to the Corinthian church, they could not pick up their New Testament and read the Gospel accounts of Jesus's death and resurrection. The Gospels did not yet exist. Paul's Corinthian letter, written sometime between AD 50 and 60, with its references to the appearances of the risen Christ, was the earliest written testimony to the resurrection. Remember that Jesus was crucified around AD 30. The Gospels of Mark, Matthew, and Luke and the book of Acts were written sometime between AD 60 and 75. John's Gospel, which was written much later, and the other New Testament writings were likely written from 90 to 125. Paul's letter would be the first written reference to those who had seen the risen Lord, but it was based on oral tradition and sketchy notes that some of the disciples had probably made. Paul had not originated the tradition but handed on to the Corinthians what was considered the early creed of the church—Christ crucified, dead, buried, and risen again.

According to the Scriptures

Paul also noted that what he proclaimed to them was according to the Scriptures (1 Cor 15:4). The early church believed that Jesus was raised on the third day. On the road to Emmaus, the risen Christ reminded two of his disciples, "Thus it is written, that the Christ should suffer and on the third day rise from the dead" (Luke 24:46). Although it is difficult for us to know exactly which Scriptures the early church read as predictions that Jesus would rise again, several could have been in their minds. In the Suffering Servant passage in Isaiah 53:1-12, the writer foretells the triumph of the Messiah. Various psalms are quoted in the New Testament to show the fulfillment of prophecy, such as Psalm 2:1, quoted in Acts 4:25-26; Psalm

16:8-11, quoted in Acts 2:25-28; Psalm 110:1, quoted in Acts 2:34-35; and Psalm 118:22, quoted in Acts 4:11. Another likely passage from the prophets is Hosea 6:2: "After two days he will revive us; on the third day he will raise us up, that we may live before him." As the new Israel, Christ fulfills the destiny of the nations. Jesus drew on the image from Jonah 1:17 when he declared, "For as Jonah was three days and three nights in the belly of the whale, so will the Son of Man be three days and three nights in the heart of the earth" (Matt 12:40). Although the disciples heard these kinds of references from Jesus, they did not understand their meaning until after the resurrection.

Death, Burial and Resurrection

Paul then summed up the content of the gospel in three short affirmations: "Jesus died, was buried, and was raised on the third day." Jesus was dead. There was no question in the disciples' minds about that. He had been flogged by Roman soldiers, nailed to a cross, and had a spear thrust into his side to make certain he was dead. The soldiers verified that he was dead before they took him down from the cross. He was then buried in the borrowed tomb of Joseph of Arimathea. He was wrapped in a mummy-like fashion, a cloth covered his face, and his body was overlaid with one hundred and fifty pounds of spices. Then the heavy, flat stone, shaped like a large wheel on an ox cart, was rolled into the track in front of the tomb entrance. It was sealed shut, and Roman guards stood watch outside the entrance. Jesus was indeed dead and buried.

Theories to Deny the Resurrection

Various theories have been set forth to deny the reality of the resurrection of Jesus. Several are listed below.

The Disciples Stole Jesus's Body

The earliest theory to try to disprove the resurrection of Jesus was proposed by the Jewish chief priests, who claimed that the disciples of Jesus had stolen his body (Matt 28:11-13). This fraudulent theory was restated recently in the novel *The Passover Plot* by Hugh Schonfield. Imagine the disciples of Jesus stealing his body and being willing to die for a lie! It seems too incredulous to be convincing that the disciples, who had been shattered by despair and defeat when Jesus died, were suddenly transformed and given new courage when they stole his body. If the disciples stole his body and later buried it, why did they not come back and reverence his grave and make it a sacred place? The disciples were not rallied by a lie. That is nonsense!

Jesus Fainted on the Cross

Others have conjectured that Jesus merely fainted on the cross and did not really die. This theory claims that Jesus fell into a coma at the end of the sixth hour and was revived later after he was taken down from the cross and placed in his tomb. The Gospels state emphatically that Jesus died. He was flogged, nailed to the cross, pierced with a spear, and was buried. Dead! Buried! He did not swoon. He was dead!

The Women Went to the Wrong Tomb

Still others have suggested that the women who came to anoint Jesus's body on Easter morning went to the wrong tomb. As the women approached the garden, perhaps they were busy talking and, in their confusion, headed to the wrong tomb and found it empty. But the Bible says that when the angel told them, "He is not here. Come, see the place where they laid him," the women became afraid and fled (Matt 28:5-8). Having been told that Jesus was buried in the tomb of Joseph of Arimathea and that Roman soldiers were guarding it, how could the women go to the wrong place? Did Peter and John also go to the wrong tomb? Whose grave clothing was found in an empty tomb? The soldiers and the priests both claimed that the stone had been rolled away from the grave where Jesus was buried.

The Disciples Hallucinated

Another attempt to disprove the resurrection has been the theory that the emotional strain of the death of Jesus and the disciples' strong desire to believe that he would live again caused them to hallucinate. It is hard to conceive of five hundred people hallucinating at one time. Maybe one person! Is it possible for the twelve disciples or crowds of people to hallucinate together? We have to remember that the disciples were not looking for Jesus to reappear, nor did they really believe that he would rise from the dead. If any of these theories are accepted, the Christian religion would be founded on a delusion.

The Resurrection Appearances of Jesus

Paul claims that the church is not a memorial society but is built on the resurrection of Christ. The resurrection is the solid foundation of the Christian church. Listen to Paul's declaration concerning the appearances of the risen Christ. In his Corinthian letter he lists six resurrection appearances of Christ. There are only ten or eleven recorded in the Gospels, Acts, and Paul's letters. Paul states that Jesus first appeared to Peter, then to the Twelve, then to more than five hundred people at one time, to James, to all the apostles with Thomas present, and finally to Paul himself.

The Gospels state that Jesus first appeared to three women, among them Mary (Mark 16:9; Matt 28:1-10; John 20:11-18). Why didn't Paul include women on his list? Women did not count for much as witnesses in that day, so it's possible that Paul did not want people to think that the church's faith was based on what were then perceived as the idle tales of women. He wanted to use what he thought would be the strongest appeal possible. People might discount the experiences of women. Yet the Gospel writers record that women were the first to see the risen Lord.

The second recorded appearance of Christ occurred on Easter afternoon as two disciples of Jesus were on their way to Emmaus (Mark 16:12-13; Luke 24:13-35). He appeared also to the disciples by the Sea of Tiberius (John 21:7-14), on a mountain in Galilee (Matt 28:16-20), and on Mt. Olivet just before his ascension (Luke 24:50). Are these last two appearances the ones Paul means when he refers to Jesus's appearing to more than five hundred at once? In the book of Acts, Luke states that Jesus "presented himself alive after his passion by many proofs, appearing to them during forty days, and speaking of the kingdom of God" (Acts 1:3). In one of his sermons, Peter stated that Jesus was crucified and killed, "but God raised him up, having loosed the pangs of death, because it was not possible for him to be held by it" (Acts 2:24).

Why Did Jesus Not Appear to His Enemies?

Some have asked why Jesus did not appear to his enemies. Wouldn't that have been better? If we were in charge, we would have had Jesus come back before the high priest and say to him, "Do you want to try again? You thought you had me, didn't you?" Or we would have Jesus slip up behind Caiaphas, the high priest, and say, "Boo! Guess who?" We would shock or frighten our enemies into believing. Jesus never attempted to convince people to follow him out of terror or by trying to dazzle them. Remember that Jesus warned his disciples, "If they do not hear Moses and the prophets, neither will they be convinced if someone should rise from the dead" (Luke 16:31).

The person like an enemy who Jesus appeared to was Paul. While Paul was traveling on the road to Damascus to persecute Christians and put them to death, Christ appeared to him. Evidently there was already fertile soil in the mind of Paul regarding Jesus, because when Jesus confronted him in a blinding light on the Damascus Road, Paul's life was forever changed.

The Manner of Jesus's Resurrection

How did Jesus rise from the dead? This answer is not revealed in the New Testament. We are told only that God raised him up. When Peter and John went into Jesus's tomb, they did not find that the spices weighing down the body had been hastily dislodged, as if somebody had tried to remove the body quickly (John 19:39). Jesus's grave clothes were still on the tomb slab. The words in Greek describe these linens as if the body inside them had evaporated or undergone a metamorphosis. The cloth that had lain over Jesus's face was rolled up on the stone slab. For Peter and John, the shape of the grave clothes was a convincing sign of the resurrection of Christ (John 20:2-10). Some kind of transformation had taken place. His physical body had become a spiritual body.

Many questions fill our minds about the resurrection. What happened to the body of Jesus? Where did Jesus get the clothes he was wearing later since his grave clothes or wrappings were left in the tomb? We do not know! What kind of body did he have? We do not know! Nevertheless, he had a body. Following the resurrection, there were appearances of Jesus in which he ate and drank with his disciples (Luke 24:36-43) and was seen walking on the shore by the Sea of Tiberius (John 21:1-14). He also made his presence known by appearing behind locked doors, disappearing from sight, and appearing in different places across many miles (John 20:19-29; Luke 24:28-50). How was this possible? We do not know! The New Testament does not attempt to answer these questions.

Leslie Weatherhead has suggested an interesting simile that might help explain what happened to the body of Jesus. He discussed his thoughts with a professor of physics at an English university. He suggested that we imagine we are holding a lump of wax in our hand. On a cold day the wax will be hard. If you heat the wax enough, it will become a liquid. If you heat it even more, it will become a gas. By heating the wax, one increases the speed of the molecules that compose the wax. Whether the wax is a solid, liquid, or gas is determined by the speed of the molecules. Weatherhead suggested that it is conceivable that Christ may have acted upon his body in such a way "as to alter the molecular speed and make the body take gaseous form in an unusually short time."[2]

Is it not possible that God could take the molecules of the Son's body and transform them in a manner that we cannot begin to perceive? Richard Rohr says his theology professor in seminary thought that the resurrected Christ would not have been seen as a lone man emerging from a grave, which would be more like resuscitation than resurrection, but instead he might have been "captured something like beams of light extending in all directions."[3] However the resurrection of Christ took place, the New Testament clearly affirms that the body of Christ was transformed and raised. The Gospels declare that his birth was a miracle, and the resurrection was also a miracle. The resurrection is the grand miracle on which our religion is based. It completed the miracle of the incarnation—God's unique entrance into the world through Jesus Christ.

What Happens if the Resurrection Is Not the Basis for Christian Faith?

Our Preaching Is in Vain

Paul argues that if the resurrection of Christ is denied, our whole basis for believing is undercut. First, he says, if people do not believe that Christ has been raised, our preaching is in vain. Paul and the other Christians had preached that Christ was raised from the grave and that people could find redemption and eternal life through a living Lord. The resurrection of Christ was the foundation on which they based their preaching. The resurrection was the transforming factor in the faith of the early disciples. They were eyewitnesses of the resurrection. They believed it because of their personal experiences with the risen Lord. His death and resurrection filled their preaching. If Christ were not risen, their preaching was based on a lie, and they had no right to preach such a delusion. But Christ has been raised from the dead, Paul exclaims, and our preaching bears testimony to that reality.

Our Faith Is in Vain

Continuing his argument, Paul declares that if Christ has not been raised, then people's faith is in vain. If we do not believe Jesus has been raised from the grave, our faith is empty, futile, and hopeless. Instead of standing on a rock, we are positioned on quicksand. There is no solid foundation. Without the resurrection, everything in our belief tumbles. If Christ were not raised, all the teachings of the church about his self-sacrifice and his life given for us are a farce. Jesus himself had consistently foretold that he would be rejected, put to death, and rise on the third day (Mark 8:31; 9:31; Matt 16:21; 20:19; Luke 9:22; 11:29). He even used the story of Jonah in the belly of a whale for three days and nights as a sign of his resurrection (Matt 12:40). If the resurrection is not a fact, then Jesus was either lying or deluded. His sacrificial death and resurrection formed the basis for much of his teaching and actions. Christ has been raised, and therefore our trust is assured.

We Misrepresent God

Third, Paul goes even further. "If Christ has not been raised," he says, "then we misrepresent God." In their preaching, Paul and the other Christians had declared that God was like Jesus—caring, loving, suffering, redemptive, and sacrificial. The resurrection was seen as an act of God vindicating the life and ministry of Jesus. The New Testament usually states that Jesus "was raised from the dead" (Acts 4:10; 10:40; 13:37; Rom 4:24; 10:9; 1 Cor 6:14; Col 2:12). If God did not raise Jesus Christ from the grave, then the early church misrepresented God. They lied about God's actions. Paul declared forcefully, however, that Christ has been raised! Our preaching, faith, and view of God are not based on a lie.

The resurrection of Christ has enabled us to see God as we had never perceived God before, but it has also provided us with a new perspective from which we can see ourselves. We see God as loving and redemptive. We see ourselves as forgiven sinners with a new beginning for our lives. The resurrection has affirmed that what Jesus taught us about God and ourselves is true. In the presence of the living Lord, we see ourselves differently.

Robert Raines tells about an interesting experience a friend had when she received a leather case. It contained handwritten instructions from her grandmother that the case be sent to her granddaughter upon her death. As Robert's friend opened the case, she discovered that it contained everything she had ever sent her grandmother: birthday greetings in the hand of a five-year-old; crayoned hearts on Valentine's Day; her first school picture; personal letters from a thirteen-year-old, and more. As she looked at herself through the eyes of her grandmother, it was an eerie and solemn occasion.

"I suddenly realized," she said, "that in preparation for her leave-taking my grandmother had arranged to send her part of my life back to me; she was giving back to me all that she loved about me—only better because she was now part of it. As I sit now pondering these things, I realize anew how she had left me alone to give witness to what we had once shared together. I am a witness for her, for myself, for our friendship. And I know that in some inexplicable way, marked by the deepest sadness, the greatest joy, and a bundle of old letters, I have been made a new person through the gift I received from her."[4]

Easter is the time when we remember again what possibilities God has seen within us, God's hopes and dreams for us, God's guidance and love, concern and grace. Easter reminds us of the God who made life good and wants us to see ourselves through God's eyes—as children created in God's image. Easter calls us to remember whose we are and what we can be. Easter is a witness to the love and power of God and the assurance of the new creation we can be through Christ, our living Lord.

We Remain in Our Sins

If Christ has not been raised, Paul continues to argue, we are still in our sins. Paul and others had preached that the death of Christ on the cross brings redemption, ransom, and forgiveness. The death of Christ would be futile without the resurrection. If Christ were not raised, we would still be burdened with our sins. Without the resurrection, we are broken under our load of sin and suffering, and we end in despair. Paul cries, Christ has been raised!

In 1926 Ford Madox Ford wrote a novel titled *A Man Could Stand Up*. The title reflects the reaction soldiers had when the armistice was signed, bringing an end to World War I. The soldiers had crouched endlessly in trenches for fear of being mowed down by machine-gun fire. Armistice Day was the time when a man felt he could now stand up without fear of being shot. If you take that same thought into the spiritual realm, you might say that the resurrection of Christ has had such a profound effect on men and women who have been trapped in the trenches of sin and defeat: Christ has set them on their feet again. The power of the risen Christ enables us to stand up as forgiven people. We know that we are not still in our sins because Christ is risen.

No Hope without the Resurrection

"If Christ has not been raised," Paul continues, "then those who have died, have died hopeless, and without any possibility of life after death." If Christ has not been raised, there is no hope for any of us.

Our hope in life after death is based on the assurance of his resurrection. To deny the resurrection of Christ is to make our Lord a liar, too. "In my Father's house are many rooms," Jesus promised. "If it were not so, would I have told you that I go to prepare a place for you?" (John 14:2). The New Testament boldly declares that all who die in Christ will live again.

"If a man or woman dies, will he or she live again?" That is the question of all people. In the novel *Magnificent Obsession*, written by Lloyd Douglas, one of the characters acknowledges that he is getting older and muses about life and whether or not it is the end.

> I've always shied off from the subject. . . . But, of late, it has been much on my mind. I'm quite disturbed these days. I'm in a mental revolt against death. It's sneaking up on me, and there's nothing I can do about it. Death holds all the trump cards. . . . It takes me a little longer to get out of bed in the morning than a month ago. It is just a bit harder to climb the stairs than it was last week. The old machine is running down. I don't want to die. I understand that when a man actually faces up to it, nature compounds some sort of an anesthesia which numbs his dread and makes it seem right enough; but that thought brings me small comfort. I have been accustomed to meeting all my emergencies with my eyes open, and I don't get much consolation out of the thought that I'm to be doped into a dull apathy—like a convict on the way to execution—as I face this last one. . . . I wouldn't mind so much if there was anything—after that. . . . Bobby, do you believe in immortality?[5]

Is there life after death? The Christian affirms that if a man or woman dies in Jesus Christ, he or she will live again. This is the great affirmation of the Christian faith: because Christ lives, we too shall live. Death is not the end for the Christian but a time of birthing from the physical world to the spiritual, from the mortal to the immortal, from the perishable to the imperishable. Death is swallowed up in victory (1 Cor 15:51-55).

Three Witnesses to the Resurrection

On Easter Sunday morning two thousand years later, we join the voices of millions of other Christians and exclaim, "Hallelujah. Christ is risen!" With Paul, we affirm that the resurrection of Christ is the foundation of the Christian church. It was the one thing—the only thing—that could have turned the defeated, despairing disciples into crusading evangelists for the gospel of Christ.

There are three great witnesses to the resurrection of Jesus Christ. The first witness is the Christian church itself. The resurrection was what founded the church. If Jesus Christ had not been raised from the grave, there would never have been a church. The church came into existence because of the disciples' belief in the risen Lord. The New Testament is the second greatest witness. The New Testament did not create the church. Disciples in the early church wrote the Gospels, Acts, and the rest of the New Testament to tell others about Jesus Christ, the risen Lord. The third notable witness to the reality of the resurrection is that the Jewish disciples changed their day of worship from Saturday, the Sabbath, to Sunday, the resurrection day. Because the Sabbath was such a sacred day for the Jews, only a miracle could make them change their day of worship from Saturday to Sunday. They declared that this miracle was the resurrection of Jesus. If the crucifixion and death of Jesus were the end of his life and ministry, then neither the church nor the New Testament would have come into existence. The resurrection made the difference!

Following the Nuremburg War Crime Trials, a witness testified that he avoided the gas chambers and survived by living for a time in a graveyard in Wilma, Poland. While he lived there, a young woman gave birth to a boy. When the child uttered its first cry, the old man prayed, "Great God, hast thou finally sent the Messiah to us? For who else than the Messiah Himself can be born in a grave?" A few days later, however, when he saw the baby sucking only the tears of his mother who was unable to give him milk, he knew that this hope would not be realized.[6]

But the Christian message is that the Messiah did come from a graveyard. Death could not contain him. The power of God raised Christ from the grave. As Paul said, "Our faith is based on the resurrection. If Christ was not raised, then everything else we believe tumbles. But thanks be to God he is risen." Let the trumpets sound! Let our voices shout, "He is risen indeed!"

Chapter 16

Now Concerning the Offering

1 Corinthians 16:1-3

A young minister was at his first church, and the time came for the morning offering. As the deacons came forward to receive the offering, he meant to say, "As our Lord has said, 'It is more blessed to give than receive,'" but he nervously said instead, "A fool and his money are soon parted." I suppose both are true in a sense. One may be more biblical than the other, though I think that in some ways both are very biblical.

When it comes to talking about a Christian and their money, many folks become uncomfortable, and they had rather not hear much said on that subject for a number of reasons. One reason is that those who are most uncomfortable with such discussions are usually those who give the least to the church. Sometimes those of us who may give more are still uncomfortable when we realize the high expectations that the Gospels have for us in this area. Off Vancouver there is a spot called "The Zone of Silence." When a ship enters this area, it cannot receive any sound to warn it of the depth of the waters because the zone is acoustically dead. Many ships have ended up on the rocks because they could not hear the sounds to warn them of the dangers.

I am convinced that a lot of people live in the zone of silence when it comes to stewardship in our churches. In this area, we are acoustically dead. We do not want to hear what the Scriptures declare about our giving. Some say, "Well, you really ought not to talk about money in church. The preacher ought to stay out of those kinds of things because, after all, that is my private business and not any of his."

This was certainly not true of the Apostle Paul. In 1 Corinthians 15 he wrote about one of the central doctrines of the Christian faith—the resurrection. We have to remember that there were no chapter divisions or verses when Paul wrote this letter. These were added centuries later. Without a moment's hesitation, he moved from writing about the resurrection of Christ to saying, "Now concerning the offering . . . ."

From a profound discussion on the resurrection, he moved immediately to writing about the offering. Without a blink of his eye and without sensing a bit of difficulty, he spoke about both because in his mind the two were meshed together. The Christian faith is not totally abstract, unrelated to life and money. Our faith is very much involved with our possessions.

Spiritualize the Material

Paul was one of those Christian preachers who kept both feet on the ground. Even when he was talking about the resurrection, he could immediately turn and write about a Christian and their money. I think one of the reasons Paul could do this is because he had learned to spiritualize the material. Many people in his day, especially the Greeks, thought that the material body and anything else material was evil. Since the human body was evil from its creation, a person wanted to escape his body and become pure. Even touching certain things could make one impure. But the Christians, on the other hand, spoke about the human body as the temple of the Holy Spirit. The human body was seen as the habitation of God. God had created the universe, and upon looking at creation God didn't say, "It's bad, it's awful." God looked at creation and said, "It is good."

Who owns the earth? Who really possesses the creation that God called good? The Communists say it belongs to the workers. The Socialists say it belongs to the state. The Capitalists say it belongs to those who have enough enterprise and expertise to handle it. Who owns the earth? All of these groups are basically wrong because the earth is the Lord's, and we are all stewards of every single thing we have on the earth. We literally do not own any of it. It is a gift to us from God. We are challenged to use the gift effectively. To do this, we need to learn to spiritualize the material. We need to learn to see within the material realm the deeper dimension of its possibility of being utilized for God's grace. Our possessions can possess us, or they can become a means to a selfish end. Our possessions can dominate our lives, and materialism can become the ultimate goal for us. Unfortunately, too many people have been caught up in that approach to life. But our possessions should never be an end in themselves. They should always be seen as a means to some greater goal in our lives. "Lay not up for yourself treasures on earth," Jesus said, "where moth and rust can corrupt, but lay up for yourself treasures in heaven" (Matt 6:19-20). How do we do that? We do that by learning to utilize material things in a spiritual way. We are challenged to use our money, possessions, and whatever we have in ways that glorify God and keep us from becoming entrapped by material things.

I had a brief acting career when I was in high school. I took a bit part in a play by James Barrie titled *The Will*.[1] In this play, a young couple comes to a lawyer because they want to make their will. They have just gotten married, are very much in love, and life is wonderful and marvelous. The husband Philip Ross, of course, wants to leave everything to his wife and suggests that the will have only one sentence to state this. But she will have none of that. She urges him to leave some of it to his cousins and a convalescent home. They both seem so much in love and unselfish. Twenty years later, they come back to the lawyer's office. Philip Ross has now become quite prosperous. Mrs. Ross comes with him to make sure he does not do anything foolish. This time there is much bickering between them, and each speaks about "my" money. The home is excluded. Twenty more years pass. Ross is now sixty-five, and his wife is dead. He comes back to the attorney to draw up his will again. He decides that he will not leave any of his money to his relatives, including his children, because they don't deserve to be remembered. As he walks back and forth trying to decide what he will do with his money, he declares, "I leave it—I leave it—my God, I don't know what to do with it!" He moves around anxiously until finally he shouts angrily,

"Here are the names of half a dozen men that I fought to get my money. I beat them. Leave it to them with my curses." Here is a man whose material goals became an end in themselves, and they ended up as a curse and not a blessing. We need to learn to spiritualize the material.

Materialize the Spiritual

We also need to materialize the spiritual. Paul did not try to keep his discussion about the resurrection in abstract thought. He used an earthy metaphor to talk about the resurrection and eternal life. He compared death and resurrection to the planting of grain in the ground. He noted how the seed decomposes and then is transformed as it comes up through the ground. You and I must learn to materialize the spiritual and not keep God in some abstract place, unrelated to life. We should avoid saying, "Well, that's for heaven" or "That is the spiritual dimension of life." The Christian faith involves both. One cannot separate the spiritual life from one's total life. The spiritual and material are a unit. What we do with our money affects our spiritual life, and how we live spiritually should affect what we do with our possessions. They are interlocked.

A man called Simon Stylites lived back in the Middle Ages. He wanted to be a spiritual man. He built a platform about thirty feet off the ground, and he lived for thirty years on that platform. He never came down but spent his life there in meditation. People would send food and clothing up to him. He was striving to be spiritual, living up there unrelated to others and uncontaminated by the world, but unknown to him, he was also being very unchristian. Jesus never meant for us to remove ourselves from the world in that sense. He meant for us to be the salt, the light, and the leaven in the world. We are to touch the material dimension of the world and transform it with our spiritual light and life.

William Temple, a famous English theologian, once said that the Christian faith is "the most avowedly materialistic of all the great religions."[2] Christianity doesn't reject, ignore, or deny the material world. It says that God created the material world and that the word became flesh. God became incarnate. God came into the world in a unique way and became involved in it and is not abstract from it. The material life is very much involved in our spiritual life. The Christian faith is not concerned merely with swell ideals or pious abstract contemplations.

A number of years ago in Mexico there was an earthquake that split a church in half. The cross that had been hanging in the back of the church fell into all the rubble. One day someone came by the ruined church and saw the cross lying on the ground. They picked up the cross and carried it into the small town and planted it in the ground in the marketplace. In a real sense, that is where the cross belongs. It should stand in the marketplaces of life, in our homes, in our businesses, in the middle of our lives. The God we worship has become involved in our lives, not separated or isolated from them. God is here in our world. The material is spiritualized by the presence of the living God in our world.

Notice what Paul says in this passage about the offering. He is primarily concerned with the offering to be collected for the Jerusalem church, which seemed to be in a bad financial condition. He urged the Corinthians to take up an offering to assist them. At first he felt that some of his helpers, Timothy, Apollos, or some others, might take the offering, but he was willing to go himself, and ultimately that is what happened. Paul did take the offering to Jerusalem.

Principles in the Use of Offerings

Paul mentions some interesting principles that we can use today concerning our own offering. First, *when* is the offering supposed to be collected? The offering should be received on the first day of the week when the church gathers together on Sunday. That is the time to give. I have always had a practice, whether I received my paycheck weekly, twice a month, or monthly, to give every Sunday. This keeps my offering as a part of my worship. Giving is a part of worship. My offering is one way I attempt to honor God. Second, *who* is to give? Each person is to put something aside. Giving is not reserved just for the wealthy; every single Christian is to do their part. Notice, third, that Paul also tells us *where* we are to give. "Store it up," he says. Most likely the storehouse is the church. The place for the focus of our giving is the church. We are charged with benevolent work so we can honor God and carry out the ministry of Christ to the needy.

Fourth, *how much* are we to give? Paul explains this clearly. As God has prospered us, we give accordingly. That doesn't mean that the poorest person in the church should give as much as the wealthiest person. As God has prospered us, we give proportionately. For Paul, talk about proportion meant the tithe. In the Jewish tradition, there was a long history of returning a tithe unto God.

Fifth, *why* are we to give? When Paul came to visit later, he did not want to gather the believers together and have to beg for more money. There is nothing more tragic than having to beg Christian people to give money for the cause of Christ. Paul says that we should give generously so the church should not have to beg for support. These simple principles seem valid today.

Attitudes toward Giving to the Church

What are some attitudes church members sometimes take toward giving to their church?

We face many temptations when it comes to giving for the cause of Christ. One of them is *aloofness*. "I am not going to get involved in that. I will just sit back and watch what other folks do." In this case, a person is aloof from all that is going on. They stand above it. Other people are *indifferent*. They choose not to get involved. "After all," they say, "I have given my dollar a week for a long time. I am not going to get involved. I will just be indifferent and wait and see what happens." Still others will *criticize*. It is easy to criticize the pastor, church committees, or other church members. It is easy to criticize why something hasn't been done the way we want it. We can't control many of the things others do, so it is easy to fall into the temptation of criticism and refuse to give.

There is also the temptation of *ridicule*. Some people begin to ridicule what one group may have done at church, or they ridicule a leader or make fun of others or their ideas. Some fall into the temptation of *impatience*. They become so tired of waiting for a goal to be realized. "It has been so long," they say. "When will we ever complete this project?" Impatiently, they criticize and ridicule because they are tired of waiting. Another temptation is to fall into *discouragement*. Words of discouragement can filter quickly through a congregation and hurt its spirit. Discouragement always arises when the times get difficult, and the end seems evasive.

Finally, we can be tempted by *good intentions*. "I mean to do this," we say, "and one of these days I'm going to get around to it." We have great intentions. It is one of our worst temptations. I read about a young boy who came to school with a huge paper bag in his hand. The teacher wondered what he had in it because it looked like an enormous lunch. The boy held on to the top of his bag until lunchtime. Finally, the teacher could stand it no longer, and she went over and asked the young boy, "What's in your bag?" The young boy replied, "Blew." She said, "Beg your pardon. What's in your bag?" He repeated, "Blew. I just blew into it." There are a lot of people who walk around with bags of "blew"! They have a lot of hot air called good intentions that they puffed up to fill "wish bags," but they are not actually going to do anything. Sometimes we are all talk but no action.

We can fall into all kinds of temptations and give way to them, or we can begin to see the worthy reasons that we should support the church. Much is happening in our churches that is worthy of our gifts and support. The majesty of worship in our churches is worthy of our gifts. The music programs and varieties of ministries are worth our giving. The Sunday school ministries, the small group studies, and the many learning opportunities in our churches are worthy of our gifts. The staff who work with children, youth, music, education, administration, counseling, and all the other areas are worthy of our support because of the fine work they do. The multitude of ministries we have through our mission organizations are worthy of our giving. The weekday ministries that we have in many of our churches, like the preschool, daycare, counseling, job center, and many others, are worthy of our giving. Each of us should be excited about the opportunities that are ours to give.

Our churches are worthy to receive our gifts when we realize how some groups use the gifts we give through certain programs. Though there are many valid ministries on television, some of these consume a lot of our money with few real ministries to show for it. When some of the television "evangelists" were at their height, in one year Oral Roberts received fifty million dollars, Pat Robertson fifty-eight million, Jim Bakker of the PTL Club fifty-one million, Jerry Falwell fifty million, Billy Graham thirty million, Rex Humbard twenty-five million, Robert Schuller sixteen million, and Herbert W. Armstrong sixty-five million. All of these total 355 million dollars. What do these TV evangelists support? The answer is three churches, five schools, one hospital, and lots of television at an enormous cost.

I believe that far more effective ministries are done through many of the various denominational programs than any television evangelist, and I encourage my church to support these offerings. It's a shame that so much money is often given to television evangelists that could be used in a far greater way through our denominational programs.

I am giving my money through my local church. I know where this money goes locally, and I know what it supports through my denomination's Cooperative Baptist Fellowship ministry. We have a great opportunity to serve Christ through our local church and its ministries and through the CBF. Colleges and seminaries I attended and other groups have asked for large sums to support their work. I will usually share a small gift with them, but my local church is my first commitment for my gifts, and I hope it will be your first commitment as well.

We are in a time of great challenge for the church today. It is easy to sit back and do nothing. But the church has a tremendous vision that we received from Christ, and I hope each of us will continue to be caught up in that vision. I hope we will give to match our vision—both to support our local ministries and to support worldwide ones. You can tell what is important in a person's life when you look at their bank account. I hope that our expenditures will indicate that we think spiritual things are of first importance. I hope you will let your church be the primary source through which you give your gifts to serve Christ.

Giving Is a Vital Part of Worship

Giving is not a side issue; it is at the center of our worship. Our giving is a reflection of our deeper commitment to God. Helen Hayes, in her autobiography titled *A Gift of Joy*, says that she was riding on a train one time and was asked if she would come back and speak with a woman who was dying.[3] The famous actress went into this woman's compartment, and the woman, who could not get out of her bed. While Helen Hayes was talking with this woman, the ailing woman nodded to her maid to get out a box of jewels. She reached over and took out some gems and held them up to the light to show off the sparkling colors. For an hour and a half, Helen Hayes said she put on the most marvelous performance of her life as she tried to act as though she were interested in what the person showed her. As this woman lay dying, all she had to show for her life were pieces of jewelry that admirers had given her. As she lay dying, her whole life was wrapped up in diamonds and gems. Miss Hayes said she wanted to cry. It is sad for a person to end her life this way.

How tragic it is that too many of us end up focusing only on material things, and we do not let these things direct us to God. Paul has reminded us that the offering is related to our spiritual lives because it is a reflection of our deeper commitment to God. I hope that my giving and yours will indicate that we are deeply committed to God.

Afterword

Paul's epistle to the Corinthian church, centuries old, still addresses some of our present sins, social and ethical issues, basic beliefs, and avenues of meaningful living. Christians and other religious seekers can find in these chapters rich guidelines in how to confront contemporary issues, interpret and proclaim basic beliefs, note patterns for worship, and sense the assurance of the Spirit's work in the world. When many political and religious leaders in our society make false claims or share untruths or speak distorted pronouncements, it is apparent that moral standards and ethical values are needed, like those affirmed in Paul's epistle. They are needed today as much as they were when the epistle was originally written.

In my opinion, without question, Paul's letter directs us to the high road in the midst of religious disagreements and the ethical and social challenges that confront us. Paul continues to challenge us to seek this high road by living a life that strives to model itself after the Christ-like way. The Christ-like way guides us to the highest principled character and moral standards we can reach for. This way is not the easy way, but it is the way that directs us in how to love our neighbors and ourselves as Christ taught us.

In a day that longs for a word of hope in a catastrophic time, struggles to preserve moral standards in an immoral age, and strives after courageous living in the midst of apathy, this ancient letter still provides direction and assurance. I believe that Paul's letter to the church at Corinth offers to readers today a powerful resource for our present moment. I continue to be grateful for Paul's gracious words written so long ago. I hope readers will likewise be enriched by studying this marvelous letter from the Apostle Paul.

Notes

Chapter 1

1. Stephen T. Um and Justin Buzzard, *Why Cities Matter: To God, the Culture, and the Church* (Wheaton, IL: Crossway, 2013), 15.

2. Helmut Thielicke, *Being a Christian* (Philadelphia: Fortress Press, 1979), 36–37.

3. Charles Paul Conn, *Making It Happen* (Old Tappan, NJ: Fleming H. Revell Co., 1981), 95.

4. Alan Walker, *One: The Disturber* (Waco, TX: Word Books, 1973), 33.

Chapter 2

1. From *The Courier Journal*, Louisville, KY, November 19, 1992.

Chapter 3

1. James Leo Garrett Jr., *Baptist Church Discipline* (Nashville: Broadman Press, 1962), 4.

2. Barbara Brown Taylor, *Holy Envy: Finding God in the Faith of Others* (New York: HarperCollins, 2019), 78.

Chapter 4

1. Jürgen Moltmann, *The Crucified God* (New York: Harper & Row, 1974), 1.

2. Fyodor Dostoyevsky, *The Idiot*, trans. Richard Pevear and Larissa Volockhonsky (Everyman's Library; New York: Knopf), 218.

3. Marcus J. Borg, *The Heart of Christianity* (San Francisco: Harper-Collins Publishers, 2003), 96.

4. Quoted in Harold Cooke Phillips, *Preaching with Purpose and Power*, ed. Don M. Aycock (Macon, GA: Mercer University Press, 1982), 279.

5. Emil Brunner, *The Mediator* (Philadelphia: The Westminster Press, 1957), 504.

6. In Carl Braaten, *Stewards of the Mysteries* (Minneapolis: Augsburg Publishing House, 1983), 43.

7. Isaac Watts, "When I Survey the Wondrous Cross," *Hymns for the Living Church*, ed. Donald P. Hustad (Carol Stream, IL: Hope Publishing Co., 1982), 148–49.

Chapter 5

1. John Galsworthy, *Maid in Waiting* (London: Heineman, 1931), 124–25.

2. John Ruef, *Paul's First Letter to Corinth* (Philadelphia: The Westminster Press, 1977), 51.

3. Robert Bolt, *A Man for All Seasons* (New York: Vintage Books,1962), 81.

Chapter 6

1. Lance Webb, *Disciplines for Life in the Age of Aquarius* (Waco, TX: Word Books, 1972), 67–68.

Chapter 7

1. *Revised Baptist Faith and Message*, SBC, Orlando, FL, June 14, 2000.

2. For more on the issue of homosexuality, see chapter 5.

3. For example, see Hans Conzelmann, *1 Corinthians* (Philadelphia: Fortress Press, 1975), 246.

4. J. Paul Sampley, "The First Letter to the Corinthians," *The New Interpreter's Bible*, vol. 10 (Nashville: Abingdon Press, 2002), 968. See also Jouetta M. Bassler, *1 Corinthians: The Women's Bible Commentary*, ed. Carol A. Newson and Sharon H. Ringe (Louisville: Westminster Press, 1992), 328.

5. Richard Rohr, *The Universal Christ* (New York: Convergent Books, 2019), 183.

6. For a thorough listing and treatment of women in the life of Jesus and in the early church, I would recommend two books to you: Evelyn and Frank Stagg, *Woman in the World of Jesus* (Louisville, KY: Westminster

John Knox, 1978) and Leonard Swindler, *Biblical Affirmations of Woman* (Louisville, KY: Westminster John Knox, 1979).

7. Judith Anne Bledsoe Bailey, *Strength for the Journey: Feminist Theology & Baptist Women Pastors* (Richmond, VA: Center for Baptist Heritage & Studies, 2015), 177.

Chapter 9

1. Eric Marshall and Stuart Hample (comp.), *More Children's Letters to God* (New York: Essanders Special Edition, 1967).

2. Henry P. van Dusen, *Spirit, Son and Father* (New York: Charles Scribner's Sons, 1958), 63. There are many books one can read on the Holy Spirit. I have more than two dozen books in my personal library, including William Barclay's *The Promise of the Spirit*; George Hendry's *The Holy Spirit in Christian Theology*; Dale Moody's *Spirit of the Living God: What the Bible Says about the Spirit*; Wayne Oates's *The Holy Spirit in Five Worlds*; Regin Prenter's *Spiritus Creator: Luther's Concept of the Holy Spirit*; Samuel Shoemaker's *With the Holy Spirit and Fire*; and Frank Stagg's *The Holy Spirit Today*. This does not include the many references to the Holy Spirit in my Bible dictionaries.

3. Barbara Brown Taylor, *Holy Envy: Finding God in the Faith of Others* (New York: HarperCollins, 2019), 170–71.

4. Bill Adler, *Dear Pastor* (New York: Thomas Nelson Publishers, 1980).

Chapter 10

1. Richard Rohr, *The Universal Christ* (New York: Convergent Books, 2019), 89.

2. Robin W. Lovin, "Church in an Amoral Time," *The Christian Century*, February 27, 2019, p. 29.

Chapter 11

1. Dean Ornish, *Love & Survival* (New York: Harper Collins, 1998), 1.

2. Karl Menninger, *Love Against Hate* (New York: Harcourt, Brace and Co., 1959), 21.

3. Rollo May, *Man's Search for Himself* (New York: W.W. Norton & Company, Inc., 1953), 238.

4. J. Paul Sampley, *1 Corinthians, The New Interpreter's Bible*, vol. 10 (Nashville: Abingdon Press, 2002), 956.

5. Henry Drummond, *The Greatest Thing in the World* (London: Collins, n.d.), 37.

6. E. Stanley Jones, *Victorious Living* (New York: Abingdon-Cokesbury, 1936), 341.

7. Andrew D. Lester, *Hope in Pastoral Care and Counseling* (Louisville: Westminster/John Knox Press, 1995), 69.

8. Helen Battle, *Every Wall Shall Fall* (New Jersey: Fleming H. Revell Co., 1969).

9. 1 Corinthians 13:1-13, *The New Testament in Modern English*, translated by J. B. Phillips (New York: The Macmillan Co., 1964). Gender-inclusive language is included to update this translation.

Chapter 12

1. William Baird, *1 and 2 Corinthians*. Knox Preaching Guides. (Atlanta: John Knox Press, 1980), 56.

2. Clarence Jordan, *The Cotton Patch Version of Paul's Epistles* (Piscataway, NJ: New Century Publishers, 1968), 66.

3. Robin W. Lovin, "Church in an Amoral Time," *The Christian Century*, February 27, 2019, 29.

Chapter 13

1. Leo Tolstoy, "Reading Circle: II Stones," http://tolstoy-lit.ru/tolstoy/proza/krug-chteniya/kamni.htm.

Chapter 14

1. Theodore H. Robinson, *The Epistle to the Hebrews*, The Moffatt New Testament Commentary (New York: Harper & Brothers, n.d.), 142.

2. William E. Orr and James Arthur Walther, *1 Corinthians*, The Anchor Bible (Garden City, NY: Doubleday & Co., Inc., 1976), 306.

3. Horton Davies, *Christian Worship: History and Meaning* (New York: Abingdon Press, 1957), 86.

Chapter 15

1. Ernest Becker, *The Denial of Death* (New York: The Free Press, 1973), 11ff.

2. Leslie D. Weatherhead, *The Manner of the Resurrection* (New York: Abingdon Press, 1959), 51–52.

3. Richard Rohr, *The Universal Christ* (New York: Convergent Books, 2019), 127.

4. Quoted in Floyd Thatcher, ed., *The Miracle of Easter* (Waco: Word Books, 1980), 81–82.

5. Lloyd C. Douglas, *Magnificent Obsession* (Boston: Houghton Mifflin, 1957), 231.

6. Paul Tillich, *The Shaking of the Foundations* (New York: Charles Scribner's Sons, 1948), 165.

Chapter 16

1. Published by Samuel French, Inc., in 1933.

2. William Temple, *Nature, Man and God* (London: Macmillan and Co., 1956), 478.

3. Published by M. Evans & Company in 1965.